AF207404

UNBOUNDED

UNBOUNDED

JOURNEY TO YOUR WITHIN

AARON MCCORMICK

ISBN: 978-1-7344010-0-4
Library of Congress Cataloging-in-Publication Data
McCormick, Aaron
Unbounded – Journey to Your Within / Aaron McCormick

Yellow Mountain Productions
PO Box 801448
Dallas, TX 75380

Printed in the United States of America

Contents

Introduction

W HILE SITTING IN an airport terminal on a business trip, I observed something typical to everyday life but for some reason it hit me more profoundly. There was a toddler being defiant with his mother – repeatedly grunting, scowling and pulling himself in the opposite direction.

Something inside the little guy, at the ripe old age of maybe 14 months told him he knew what he was doing — and that being forced to go in a certain direction just didn't feel right. Any parent knows this experience firsthand. Every single day the child is becoming more powerful, proficient and increasingly able to do things with less direct help, involvement or even coercion of his parents. Any time the baby in the terminal would stumble or fall he would happily reach out for the hand of his parent for the needed support rising back to his feet. Immediately after gaining control, the infant would defiantly let go and resist any further assistance.

But... when Mom shifts her attention to other things, what happens? The baby inevitably came right back around seeking to be noticed, craving eye contact and attention. The baby will not be satisfied until he knows Mom has noticed and more specifically engaged him. Yet, if the parent meddles too much he will cry, grunt and run away and the entire cycle will repeat itself. Apparently, babies crave social interaction and to affect Mom just as strongly as they crave freedom from her. They want to be seen and experienced but do not necessarily want to have their course or plans altered.

That a 14-month-old baby innately possesses the wisdom to encapsulate into 60 seconds not only the first 21 years of human life, but the entire 80-100-year journey amazed me. From our first breath until the last, we seek the balance of freedom, self-expression and actualization, coupled with stimulating interaction and support along the path we believe to be our objective and purpose.

From the moment we enter the world, there exists invisible energy or spirit that contains volumes of information. It is as if we come self-contained with a specific essence and purpose awaiting conscious revelation and fulfillment. However, more intrusive and far less constructive than loving hands trying to help us physically walk, we are barraged by ideals, expectations, labels, behavior and energy that are foreign to our original plan and essence. As the years go by, we learn to suppress, ignore or sever the direct connection to the heart that once prompted us to speak up and push back on any conflicting path, experience or energy. This prolonged suppression renders us hindered, at best, and mutated, at worst. The result is a life of perpetual internal frustration and conflict that is tear-inducing and grunt-worthy indeed! What if there were a way to rediscover your original and authentic expression, objective and purpose balanced with more positive interactions and relationships with others? How would that feel?

In a word… Unbounded!

The word "unbound" means to no longer be under restraint. However, "unbounded" expands this idea significantly and means to actually become limitless. What would it feel like to be unbounded? To catch a glimpse, you have only to think back to two situations in your life when you invested a lot of time and energy, perhaps days or even weeks. In the first situation or project, you were involved because you felt you *had* to be — you were essentially acting out of compulsion. In the other situation you were inspired, motivated and deeply committed to the work or project.

Have you allowed your imagination to fully immerse you in these experiences? Ok, now can you feel the energy you were in at the time of each scenario? Did you notice that during the project you *wanted* to do your energy is higher, you are filled with a greater sense of purpose and find the time significantly more enjoyable than the project primarily motivated by compulsion? With the absence of low vibrational energies such as fear, guilt or internal conflict you are completely engrossed. Time even gets away from you; your creativity and resourcefulness are off the charts and you feel boundless.

Doesn't it feel great! Linger in this energy for a few moments. Relax. Breathe it in. Now imagine multiplying and cascading this feeling across every important area of your life!

While this book is all about journeying to *your* "within" it is always helpful to better understand the person with whom we are communicating. My name is Aaron McCormick. No middle name, just Aaron McCormick. I was a kid raised on the southside of Chicago destined to be crippled by almost every externally imposed and therefore eventually self-imposed limitation you can imagine. We were poor; my three siblings and I raised by our single mother. I had no college education. My father exited our life when I was 3 years old and was purportedly bi-polar-schizophrenic. Although I had never personally seen behavior indicative of mental illness, I recall being concerned in my adolescence of whether I might also end up with mental illness.

The proverbial knockout blow was that I was born and raised in the mental and emotional control of extreme fundamentalist religion. Although a denomination of Christianity, that is where any semblance of normalcy ends. Virtually *any* personal development or seeking of fulfillment outside of working to further the interests of the religion was highly discouraged or outright banned. We could not participate in school sports or extra-curricular activities, or attend college, celebrate holidays or birthdays, date for fun, wear facial hair or even maintain close friendships with anyone not in the religion — and if you no longer wanted to be in the religion you are permanently cut off and considered dead to all friends and family!

Any *one* of these formidable challenges are debilitating, much less being laden with five or six! Nonetheless, I have managed to find deep personal fulfillment *along with* unprecedented secular success earning millions as a global top-performing sales executive, entrepreneur, MBA, artist, author and international speaker. To my attainment of personal and secular success and fulfillment I attribute two things: *Joy* and *Empathy.*

Though each of our journeys and challenges are unique, I am more conscientious than ever of the immense value, love and power all embody within; and how every experience, connection and inter-section serve our purpose. The question is:

To what degree will you choose to be consciously aware and intrinsically-driven?

Unbounded You

Identifying Your True Purpose

CHAPTER ONE

Identifying Your True Purpose

W HAT COMES TO your mind when you ask yourself the question: What is my purpose? If you are thinking "my family," "my business or charity," "my relationship with God or religion" are my purpose, think deeper. What is it that prompted you to even have a family, start a business/organization or seek God? *Is it not a desire to experience joy and a sense of purpose?* We see this core purpose of joy become evident by observing how infants naturally seek an experience that will bring a feeling of contentment or joy and conversely reject and protest any experience that does the opposite.

Babies are almost completely inwardly driven, their conscious mind not yet re-wired and sent on the wild goose chase of looking externally for answers that are only within. It is not just babies that are highly intuitive and inwardly focused. Our beloved mature seniors are as well. By the time we are up in age, we are under fewer delusions and less likely to be striving for more money or obsessed with impressing others. The older we get, the more we do precisely what we want to do with our time — traveling, having coffee, playing bingo, reading the paper, sitting in the park, enjoying grandchildren or a pet. It is noteworthy that at the two proverbial bookends of life — infancy and twilight — we seem to really get it.

However, it is the middle portion of our life we are adrift, experiencing self-imposed highs, lows and even crises applying much conscious thought and energy seeking the purpose of joy that once came so naturally when we were babies. Eventually, after much searching in vain to find our purpose *externally,* we slow down, turn within and the goose chase of running from ourselves ends. It makes you wonder if we have this inner "knowing" when we are babies and elderly because in both cases, we are closer to the other side. I suppose we will never know for sure until we actually die, pass on, cross over or whatever one chooses to call it.

It can be said that the original essence at birth and in infancy is our *purest* expression since it exists *before* environmental and societal conditioning and molding. Our untainted essence is sometimes referred to as the "higher-self." This is a fitting term since we just discussed how our purest expression or "purpose" is to seek and experience *joy*. Any time you see the word "purpose" in this book, you should think "joy and fulfillment". If you research emotional vibration chart, you will find lists of human emotions and their corresponding measured energy frequency. Notice that joy is near the very top. When we go within and choose to do the things that bring us joy, we are raising our vibrational frequency.

Going within, while awesome and beautiful, is *not* always easy. Why is going within and therefore *up* so hard? Looking at those same vibrational charts you will also notice many emotions that have a correspondingly *low* vibrational frequency. How many pull-ups can you do? How many feet off the ground can you jump? Just as doing pull-ups and jumping require exertion to counteract the physical law of gravity; it takes significant effort to move beyond those lower frequencies which have essentially become laws within and around us.

When we progressively move beyond being impaired or *bound* by the effects of lower vibrational emotions like fear, guilt, shame; and begin to transmute or transform them into higher vibrational emotions like Joy, Love, Appreciation, Peace and Acceptance, it is as if we are restoring and rebuilding our authentic person and aura from the inside out.

The more often we do things that place us in the higher frequency emotions, we exercise our *heart* or "purpose" muscles. Eventually we become attuned enough to immediately sense and most importantly, act whenever there is lack of resonance. When we feel internal conflict with our purpose of joy, we reject and pursue an alternate course that is in better alignment. The more we progress living in the heart, the more organic and efficient the path within and to our purpose.

The *mind* supports the process of stepping more fully into our purpose of experiencing joy when we intellectually seek to learn by doing research, reading books or taking courses. While the mind and heart both serve a purpose, it is the heart that ultimately holds the blueprint of your authentic spirit or essence. The challenge is that the heart has often been suppressed for so long that by the time the mind surrenders the reigns back to the heart, we are up in age. This is where the conscious *mind* can be a powerful ally when it questions and seeks. That you are reading a book about going 'within' indicates you have felt a prick from the *mind* prodding you to connect internal dots and open a clear connection with your heart now!

Most people want to feel happier, more fulfilled and even wealthy. However, their approach and priorities unwittingly belie their objectives leaving them striving after what therefore remains perpetually elusive — while the real answers lie untapped within. The beauty of understanding the simplicity of your original purpose of experiencing joy and fulfillment, is that this single piece of knowledge can deliver answers to virtually any dilemma or question. For example, a business owner sent this question to me:

I'm always trying to figure out how to spend more time doing creative things. Every time I get to tap the creative side and I produce something amazing, my vision expands, my energy doubles, my excitement increases, and I get even more motivated. Then the routine of day-to-day jobs and keeping the lights on knocks me off my high. How can I spend more time in the creative zone?

While this seems like a specific business question it is fundamental to every human. What to do about the urge to spend more time doing what truly makes one happy, lifts one's spirit and motivates when they also feel the trigger and pressure to earn money to keep the lights on. If the business owner were to answer his own dilemma with intrinsic awareness, his internal dialog might go something like this:

What is my purpose? To maximize my joy and fulfillment. I realize that not only has experiencing joy been my purpose since the very beginning of life, but I continue to crave such now. Hence, I will increasingly make it a priority to allocate more time to be in the creative zone which is apparently my purpose. Because I hate numbers and want to primarily be doing what I love most, perhaps I can delegate the more mundane jobs and tasks to a person who enjoys them. The idea that doing more of what I enjoy could result in lower revenue or have detrimental impact to my business is a fear base illusion. Stepping more fully into my purpose will ultimately help my business just as it helps me because my business is an extension of me. This applies to my family and relationships – a genuinely happier me is to give them a more complete me.

This same internal dialog can be applied universally. No matter the area of life, the equation works the same just played out with different characters and objects. It comes down to being either intrinsically-driven or extrinsically-driven. The intrinsic part is always represented by *you* — your purest truth, expression and aptitude for joy. The extrinsic part is represented by *everything* else; typically, money, learned ideals and behaviors, another person or group of people. The overarching question to ask yourself, therefore, becomes:

"In seeking to more fully embody my purpose of *joy and fulfillment* will I choose to live more *intrinsically* or *extrinsically?*"

Chapter two will help you personally measure how you have been doing thus far. The irony of doing more of what we love is that when it comes to work, it will often require courage and a complete shift in our mindset. For example, the small business owner may have to face a temporary decline in revenue or profit. Some may have to face ridicule from others. In other cases, the energy and prodding from within can be so strong that it requires exit from the so-called safety of a career or job to focus on what really moves the heart and soul. It could mean exiting certain relationships, religion or groups that have outwardly stood for stability or safety, yet deep down might impede the fullest expression of oneself. Only you will know the physical challenges you must face and conquer to connect with your truest expression and realize the gift *of* yourself *to* yourself and the rest of the world.

CEO You

CHAPTER TWO

CEO You

THE CHIEF EXECUTIVE Officer (CEO) is the person with the most influence and control of a corporation. One of the CEO's primary jobs is to prepare the organization for change. Unlike departmental executives, it can even be said that a CEO is nearly limitless in his or her ability to affect change for the organization.

Who have you allowed to become the CEO or boss of *your* life? When asked that question, most people quickly respond confidently, *Me, of course!* However, when answered introspectively and transparently, inevitably the real answer is another person's name, an organization, a set of ideals, social group — or even a deity!

Whatever your personal answer to this question, you are correct. However, also remember that because it is *your* life and it is *you* who assigns control, *you* are the real boss and CEO! And rightfully so, considering the interpretation and cerebral imprint of your life's experiences are 100% internal and exclusive to you. In other words, the only person that experiences your life is you! Hence, it makes perfect sense that *you* and your conscious and subconscious thoughts and energy wield the most influence and control over your life.

A fundamental difference between a corporate CEO and you is how results are measured. One is measured *extrinsically;* the other is measured *intrinsically.* The corporate CEO is primarily measured by the financial performance of an organization; whereas your definitive barometer of how well you are leading *your* life is an open and honest answer to one question:

"How happy and fulfilled am I?"

Just as the financial performance of a corporation requires the proficient and cohesive execution of each department, your fulfillment is directly attributable to how you are managing the key areas of life.

In broad terms, let's suppose the key areas that most contribute to overall happiness and fulfillment are family and social tribe, health, personal fulfillment, career, and romantic love. The volume and degree of misalignment between the *vision* we hold for ourselves in each respective category and our *reality* indicates how well we are performing in that specific area. Notice I said the vision *we* hold for ourselves. No one else can grade our personal fulfillment. All gaps or misalignment between our *vision* and our *reality* directly correlate to the amount of internal conflict we have become accustomed to accepting.

In either case — corporate or personal — the better you understand the boss, the easier it is to align with the boss's objectives, resulting in a reality that is no longer in conflict with the boss's vision. In the context of your life, the boss is you and of course the boss's purpose is joy and fulfillment. In this way, life is a journey to the within—what each of us *are* inside without dilution or alteration. When you comprehend what makes you tick and continuously heed the prodding, you experience a reality more closely aligned with the vision you hold for yourself, ultimately making you — *Unbounded.*

Why the term unbounded? Because being unbounded denotes having no limits, which is precisely how we originally experienced the world and our journey; with limitless possibilities. As a bright-eyed child with unbridled imagination, the world was destined to be whatever you dreamed and decided it would be. However, by the time we are adults the real you is unrecognizably disguised by or buried under a plethora of *binders*! Binders are both environmentally absorbed and self-administered, increase in grip over time and impede every single aspect of our lives. To better understand these binders and how they work, consider how we all enter the world. Isn't it true that we immediately possess a personality, energy, spirit, aura, or essence unique to us and un-learned? These five terms will be used interchangeably throughout this book.

Binders are various energy, thought patterns, fixed labels and behaviors that alter and impede the authentic essence diverting one further from its original purpose. Consumed and administered over time via absorption of other people's energy, learned familial, peer, and societal ideals, these binders constrict and distort how we view ourselves, our experiences, our power, *and* our possibilities. Externally absorbed energies that lack resonance within, cause deviation of purpose - things that intrinsically bring joy and fulfillment - and sometimes complete mutation of the *person*.

The result of these absorbed and self-imposed binders can be summed up by two words and applied across all aspects of life — *internal conflict*. Internal conflict is significantly worse and more detrimental to our well-being than any conflict with an external party. Internal conflict is relentless because there is no option of departure, separation, or relief. Even when our true purpose or desire is unconsciously buried under binders, and we *think* we are comfortable living with suppression, the side-effects of internal conflict inescapably reverberate across every area of your life.

The only "no conflict" policy y have is with yourself.

To disagree with your friends, secular boss, spouse, supposed race, sex, nationality, counselor or even pastor is not the end of the world. However, remaining in conflict with yourself is the end of your better world before it begins. The world or life experience in which your soul flourishes in its authentic expression increasingly attracting light, love and abundance *begins* when you stop running, start listening and surrender.

When we accept a reality alternate from our internal vision or expectation for ourselves, we in effect self-administer binders to our life experience and potential. Your conscious mind does not see it that way for the same reasons that it applied the binder and accepted the associated internal conflict in the first place — fear of displeasing other persons or entities, fear of failure, shame, the need for acceptance, and lack of awareness of our self-contained wisdom and power at a soul level.

With prolonged internal conflict, the subconscious aura kept in a state of perpetual protest due to the absence of its true purpose begins to emit excessive anxiety, low self-esteem, depression, fear, dependence, narcissism, and other imbalanced low-frequency emotions and patterns. One of the hallmarks of a great CEO is the ability to assess value and eliminate waste. Similarly, as you develop the ability to go within and eradicate the ideals, behaviors and paradigms impeding your purpose, you experience new levels of internal peace, power and fulfillment irrespective of people and outcomes that might have previously intimidated you.

Decoding What Makes You Tick

CHAPTER THREE

Decoding What
Makes You Tick

"I HAVE NO IDEA what makes them tick" is a common phrase you might hear a person lament about someone they know or love. Not surprisingly, we are often perplexed about the aura, motivations, biases and behavior of other people… after all, the majority of humans do not even know what makes *themselves* tick. How can this be? We have been ourselves for all of our lives. It should be obvious what makes us tick, no? The world would be a much happier place if that were the case! Unfortunately, however, truly understanding what makes one tick is not a 'rite of passage'. Deep insight into oneself is not necessarily acquired with the elapsing of time. While it is true, some awareness and knowledge are gleaned over time — to passively wait to learn via time alone is to bolster the cliché "youth is wasted on the young."

But what if you could "reel in" time like a fisherman reels in a catch? What if you could compress the time it might otherwise take you to grasp the breadth, height and depths of your very essence and deeply comprehend what makes you tick? If you had this ability, then it could never be said by the future "you" that *this* moment, this period of your life was 'wasted' on the young. Before you say, 'Wait, I'm not young anymore,' let me remind you that regardless of your age — you are "young" compared to what you will be in 1, 5, 10 or 20 years from now! Journeying to your within makes this possible!

The physical display of your essence became outwardly decipherable when you were as young as 1-year-old. It is as if we come self-contained with a specific essence and purpose awaiting conscious revelation, application and fulfillment.

Unaltered by "binders" or the baggage of others and society, the infant and toddler "you" holds clues about your purpose that are repeated throughout your life like breadcrumbs for you to pick up, connect the dots and decode. If you were thinking, 'But I remember nothing about being an infant or toddler,' don't worry we will address this in a later chapter.

One strong characteristic of nearly all children is curiosity and a strong desire to ask the question *'Why?'* about nearly everything!

Asking 'why?' is fundamental to growth. But what most people fail to realize is that by far *the* most powerful application of 'why?' is when directed internally. When we ask ourselves *why* we feel this way or behave that way, we not only connect with and come to understand the *real* boss better, but the ensuing growth can significantly enhance the quality of our experience almost immediately!

The objective is to train and flex our introspection and critical thinking muscles. The term critical does not mean critical in the context of criticizing. Rather, critical thinking as in more deeply pondering the cause and effect plus any associated ramifications instead of just blowing past and accepting a statement or ideal just because. Simply asking, *"Why do I feel this way about this particular person or subject?"*, *"Why do I become filled with fear or anxiety when this or that happens?"*, *"Why do I personally believe such and such?"*, starts the process of unbinding ourselves from absorbed conscious and unconscious thoughts and behaviors that are inauthentic and counterproductive to our ultimate purpose. Hence, the better you get at asking introspectively *"why?"* and willingly accepting the answers, the greater your aptitude for living out your true purpose and best life.

Why can this be said? As discussed in chapter 2 whether consciously acknowledged or not, *you* are the chief and steward of your life and all experiences. The deeper your understanding of *you* the happier and more fulfilled you will be.

This is not as easy as it sounds! You might

have heard or read that *over 90% of brain activity is subconscious.*

This implicates the vast majority of our animation — why we consciously think and act as we do — is a complete mystery to us. Hence the importance of forging a clearer connection to the heart, spirit, energy or force that is really in control. Deciding to follow the heart is like a delicately balanced proactive surrender. When we surrender, the conscious and subconscious mind no longer battle but become integrated, aligned and work in concert. What is the result? Complete freedom from internal conflict. Balance. Fulfillment. Power. Abundance. Peace. Increased love of self and others. Successful accomplishment of purpose.

In connecting within, the value of meditation should not be overlooked. However, this particular book will focus on ways to become more self-aware through conscious introspection. Stilling the mind through meditation and deliberately pursuing conscious introspection are complementary to each other. A person will either meditate thereby causing them to slow down and also become more consciously introspective, or vice versa. In either case, both are valuable to evolving from a life experience fraught with internal conflict and into a more integrated one inclusive of the outcomes you have always desired.

One of the many benefits of becoming *consciously* intrinsic is making better decisions in real-time.

Before embarking on your personal journey "within," we will do a fun warm-up exercise. This exercise will get you used to leveraging the power of "why," which will be instrumental to maximizing your purpose. We will ponder some commonly known paradoxes. A paradox is defined as a seemingly absurd or self-contradictory statement or proposition that when investigated or explained may prove well-founded or true. For example, "The more money, the more problems." Since this is a warmup, the topics are deliberately trivial. Yet it is of note that some of these may have been mentioned so often that you personally have adopted a belief one way or another without ever considering *why* you believe such. The exercise is to allow your own mind to consider why each paradox exists and ponder why it might or might not be true.

As you consider each, let your mind freely wander and eventually arrive at your *own* conclusions and perspective for each paradox *before* reading my thoughts. Write down your thoughts for each paradox.

1. The most powerful entertainers are often humble and shy offstage. Pause and ponder before moving to the next one. What are your thoughts on this paradox? Why might it be or not be so?

____

____

____

2. Some of the richest people are super nice and down to earth. Pause and ponder before moving to the next one. What are your thoughts on this paradox? Why might it be or not be so?

____

____

____

3. The most beautiful girls and most handsome guys often go lonely. Pause and ponder before moving on. What are your thoughts on this paradox? Why might it be or not be so?

____

____

____

Paradox #1 The best entertainers often seem shy and humble off stage

The reason some of the greatest entertainers are powerful on stage, field or court yet seem paradoxically humble and even shy otherwise might be attributed to a euphoric surge of energy they receive when performing. While doing their purpose, they are almost 100% in the heart space which completely transforms them albeit temporarily.

Another reason might be that they have an especially high growth mindset. Although they confidently recognize their only limitation is themselves, they also possess a humble awareness that their opportunity for greatness arose from learning from others that came before them. Furthermore, their often unparalleled work ethic indicates they likely do not feel entitled. These all seem like plausible reasons superstar performers embody both a high degree of humility *with* immense confidence and power.

By asking "why?" even on mundane topics, we not only train ourselves to think more critically but occasionally we can also grasp new lessons that might apply to our own journey. For example, while randomly analyzing the greatest performers, the following lessons might also flash across your mind:

1. Be humble enough to learn from others.

2. Aim for the moon with complete confidence you have the power to accomplish anything.

3. If your secular work is something that you are passionate about and brings you joy, the tireless work ethic required to become great will come naturally.

Imagine the lessons you might learn from doing the same thing with your personal feelings, beliefs, biases, patterns and behaviors.

Paradox #2 Some of the richest people are super nice and down to earth

It makes sense to first ponder how this paradox even came to be in the first place. The paradox rests on the basis that most affluent people are condescending snobs. I have observed, that *self-made* affluent people seem to be especially grounded, kind, hard-working people. They often come from under-privileged backgrounds and they deeply believe and have personally experienced that *everyone* has the potential to build financial wealth. They also know that they would not succeed without guidance along their journey and the direct labor of others. This imbues them with an aura of positivity, humility and appreciation — making them refreshing to be around.

Another reason for this paradox could be

expectation of negative or condescending behavior are so high that when people observe even the most basic levels of courtesy or humility it makes an exaggeratedly positive impression.

Paradox #3 The most beautiful girls and most eligible guys often go lonely

Have you ever met someone you thought was so beautiful or handsome that they must either already have a significant other or a long line of clamoring suitors; only to discover they were not only single, but they are disproportionally rarely propositioned? The reason for this paradox might be a bit more obvious than the others. Since most assume that they already have someone or have a vast array of options —they just don't bother.

As you internally pondered these paradoxes, did your perspective broadened at all? Can you see how asking yourself the simple question "why?" when it comes even to things you may have always felt or believed — can shed new light on what makes you tick?

WHY DO I FEEL THIS WAY?

My wife and I were contemplating selling our home. We loved this home. We loved its architectural style, the large yard and even how the neighborhood was small and intimate. During the five years we owned the home we had transformed it from "having potential" to becoming a "showstopper" — the personally invested blood and sweat brought additional satisfaction when coming home to it. However, we both were intrigued by the idea of doing it all over again with a different home. All data suggested that our home's value might be at its peak for the foreseeable future. We found ourselves at a crossroads. After completely renovating the home inside and out, investing several hundred thousand dollars and even welcoming our first child, we had formed a bit of an attachment to the home.

If we sold it, we could: 1) cash out 2) purchase a home with even greater upside potential or 3) enjoy additional amenities not available on our current house. While keeping a close eye on the real estate market, we found a house we loved and met all the required criteria for us to move. But there was a problem… since we were only *passively* watching the market, we had not listed our home for sale yet. We scrambled to get a real estate agent and prepare our house for sale — in less than two weeks which was record time by the way! However, by the time we were ready to list our home the other house was already under contract. To say we were bummed would be a huge understatement. We had looked at hundreds of homes in multiple surrounding suburbs before finding only *one* we liked. We had a decision to make… move forward with putting the house up for sale in hopes of finding another one in time. Or list our home for sale only after we identify a suitable replacement and do the rodeo scramble all over again.

What would you have done? When asked her preference, my wife said, 'I just want to enjoy our home and not worry about moving.' The reason her answer did not surprise me is that there was a part of me thinking the same thing. Yet as nice as our house was, we knew we were craving change and I could not stop thinking about how we found a house that ticked even more boxes.

I asked myself... '*Why* did we both initially decide to not list our home? What was the emotion that caused us to be apprehensive about stepping toward something we were *so* excited about just three days prior?' The answer became clear. We felt *fearful* of taking affirmative steps to emotionally disconnect from a great house without a currently visible backup. Although emotional detachment precedes any divestiture, we apparently wanted to have our cake and eat it too! For a woman that loves to decorate, cook and entertain to stop emotionally investing in her home without an identified replacement creates anxiety and internal conflict within her. Yet, the odds were low that both of us would stop doodling looking at other homes online. This meant it would only be a matter of time before we found ourselves in the same frustrating situation all over again; finding and missing another home we really like due to being encumbered by the sale of our house or feeling tempted to bite off more than we should chew.

By introspectively asking "why?" we learned something important. When faced with uncertainty the natural tendency to take the easier more "comfortable" path in deference to what you truly desire not only prolongs attainment of the goal but suspends you in anxiety.

When asking yourself *"why?"*, pay special attention to the resulting *feeling* or *energy* more than the words or narrative that comes into the mind. The words are the story we *want* to tell ourselves, whereas feelings are the *truth* within ourselves. Asking *"why?"* brings the two together allowing you to understand, intercept, and conquer fears holding you back from the purpose of joy that you ultimately seek. In this way, when the conscious and subconscious mind come together, the most aligned and satisfying path of cohesion devoid of internal conflict will become clear.

Unbounded Career and Business

Who's a "Boss"

CHAPTER FOUR

Who's a "Boss"

WE ARE APPROACHING the year 2020. Our society is completely obsessed with being "Boss" or living a "Boss Life" which is generally depicted by affluence, fame and/or beauty. We hear it in music lyrics, we see it in movies, on television and on social media. Even parents have become obsessed with ensuring such for their children when they grow up. Although the idea of being a "Boss" has become highly popularized, it is obviously nothing new. Since all of us were children we never wanted to be told what to do - we would rather be the one doing the ordering! Every parent has observed how from an age younger than any of us can personally remember, we wanted to be in control!

What is it that we wanted so badly to control? Our experience! The word experience is often used synonymously with *time*. For example, "Did you have a good *time?*" is the same question as "Did you have a good experience?" "I have twenty years *of experience* racing cars," is the same as "I have twenty years racing cars." While everyone is hyper-focused on obtaining as much money as possible it should be noted that *time* is worth far more than money because it is time that makes all else possible; including love. If there is any doubt time is worth more than money, just ask any billionaire how much money they would forfeit for more *time* when on their deathbed!

Logically then, the most accurate definition of a "Boss" in the pop-culture connotation must be the person doing whatever they want with their *time*. That is real wealth and abundance!

Affluent yet overworked business owners, doctors and other professionals when asked whether they were 'doing what they really wanted to do with their time' often answer with a resounding "NO." They work too many hours, wish they could spend more time at a certain hobby, with their spouse, children or desire to spend more time exercising. If enslaved by a need to conform to paradigms and ideals that control their time so much they are always in want of different utilization, would you consider that a "Boss?" If they are gripped by either an insatiable desire for more money — or a morbid fear of not having enough of it, should it be considered living a 'boss life?'

Although this desire to do what we want with

our time is intrinsic to human nature, our manifestation of such seems to devolve as we mature to adulthood. When I say it devolves, I do not mean it necessarily erodes or goes away. Rather, our desires become progressively extrinsic as we mature through childhood, teen and young adulthood. Remember intrinsic means natural and internal to our being; whereas extrinsic is foreign and external to our being. As we progress through life:

1. The things we *think* will make us happy become increasingly influenced by external sources like school peers, coworkers, pastors, TV, friends, neighbors, movies, music, etc.

2. We begin to prefer money or material things over experiences.

3. Curiosity, exploration and desire to learn and expand are replaced by apathy. Fear of looking ignorant or non-conforming stunts expansion of the mind and inner spirit.

As we approach adulthood, we are significantly less internally animated and empowered. The spark; that is the glimmer in the eye, excitement, belief, hope and personal sense of purpose has already begun to dim.

Some may say, "I work so hard so my family and I can have all the trappings I did not have and thereby enjoy our *time* more!" Think back to some period of your life when you really wanted something. You can even go back to childhood; that special baby doll, video game or toy car. What happened not long after you got it? Did it remain special to you? Of course not, it got old, didn't it? Yet *before* you got it you swore to your parents and yourself that if you got that one you would be satisfied and never need another.

When I was 20 years old, I bought my first house. It had four bedrooms a two-car garage and a huge yard. Yes, I was a little old man! I even had three cars; a Honda Accord as my daily beater, Lexus GS 300 as my business car and a Nissan 300ZX as my personal toy. I thought I was balling. And guess what; as a 20-year-old black kid on the South Side of Chicago, I was! There's just one issue. In about six months they were all old news to me. Throughout my teens, the 300Z was a car I had read about in countless magazine articles and lusted after every time I saw commercials. Owning a home was the "American Dream." Yet, in less than a year they were simply 'cars and a house'.

At approximately 21years old, it became profoundly clear to me that it would have been the same had my house been a mansion on the ocean instead of a 4 bedroom in the Suburbs of Chicago and my cars Rolls Royce and Ferrari's instead of Lexus and 300Z. I allowed this universal truth and profound lesson to deeply sink in:

No matter where it comes from oi seemingly grand, the luster never lasts.

To put it even more bluntly:

No matter where shit comes from, shit gets old!

Over the next 18 years I owned million-dollar homes and over 100 cars including many exotics. Often, I would go from an exotic car down to a simple minimalist toy because it made me smile and was 'laugh out loud' fun to drive. Every so often my friends would jokingly tease me about driving old or relatively cheap cars. At the other end of the spectrum, I would often forget how rare and 'lusted after' some of my cars were. Don't get me wrong, I appreciate how Lamborghini and Ferrari look, sound and perform — but their impact on me is much less than my first Toyota Supra and 300Z were to the 17-20 year-old me. Fortunately for me, importance placed on things has been outpaced by my expanding perspective of the world, life and what this journey is really all about. Though I appreciate well-made things and consider myself a man of taste —allowing myself to learn these lessons from a relatively young age has helped me sidestep the plague of *"undeveloped desire"*.

Undeveloped desire is desire purely fueled by the five senses with no consideration of our real purpose and the overarching paradigms at play. Our focus becomes primarily two things: gaining and maintaining approval and adoration from others and obtaining more money to indulge material possessions we have been *led* to believe will deliver joy and happiness. The illusion seems so promising the majority of people are in obsessive hot-pursuit of money and things while others are consumed by fear of either losing their money or failing to save enough of it. Regardless of the subject matter fear is crippling.

"But money drives creativity and entrepreneurship" some say. While there is some truth to this, the sad reality is money more prolifically stifles creativity and entrepreneurship. For every person whom has created value, there are millions of people whose ingenuity, authenticity and sense of purpose are suppressed while they work at a job not in alignment with their purpose of joy due to fear of lacking *money*. In other words, for every entrepreneurial success story or person who made themselves into 'something from nothing', motivated by money, there are millions who feel stifled, stay put and do nothing because of it!

Have you noticed more people are passive-aggressive? They are passive because they have lost their own compass; aggressive due to mounting frustration from not even being aware of the problem, much less a solution. Money and the things money can buy is one of the most powerful binders. When we are small children it is toys. When we get older it becomes bigger toys, houses or even just digits on a screen. Until we realize…

The person whom thinks they are a "Boss" *because* of their money and possessions are actually morbidly scared of it. The response most people give when asked if they fear money is almost always something like "no way, money is great; in fact, I would love more of it!" Yet the same majority spend most of their lives and energy in school or working at jobs they do not enjoy or even hate, to avert an outcome that *scares* them — not having enough money. Hence, they actually fear money — the lack of money to be specific. In fact, the mere idea of lacking money to enjoy life or to retire is quite triggering and painful for most to even consider. So, what do they do? They devote every bit of time, energy and more to averting such a possibility – in effect becoming a slave to the one of the most powerful *"binders"* of them all. Remember, binders are ideals, energy and behaviors which are external to our being and disruptive to our purpose of joy.

The phrase "More money, more problems" especially gets to me because as discussed in chapter 3 — if more people introspectively pondered *why* this paradox even exists they would begin living a happier and fulfilling life with or without more money!

In my early 20s I began earning hundreds of thousands of dollars annually. After seeing some outward sign of financial affluence like my car or house, people would often ask if I would teach them to do whatever I did to afford such nice things. They perceive themselves to be 'just asking for career advice or business mentoring' unaware that they have been conditioned to believe that money is the catalyst for happiness. Therefore, it is as if they are actually asking me 'how they might become happier.'

Seeking intrinsic fulfillment through material riches is an illusion.

After the basics — food, shelter, clothing, warmth — virtually no change to our physical bodies result from having yet "nicer" things. Nicer material possessions like big diamonds, nice watches, houses, cars are 100% psychological mind tricks to boost the ego and self-esteem — "I perceive I am greater and more valuable in my _mind_ — which makes me feel proud. I perceive I am more competent and successful when I have this item."

As humans with a finite lifespan, _time_ is without question the most valuable asset. Despite human ego and the insatiable desire to compete, there is no way to have more time than someone else. However, the decision to use one's time as they wish is the definition of a "Boss." Awakening to this truth early in life was at least one of the key reasons I entered sales — a profession that paid and measured me by my _perfor-mance_, not my time! I knew if I were good enough, I could earn more than most CEOs – and have more personal time to boot! I especially enjoy being in the high-vibe presence of people who do what they want with their time. These are the real bosses — for they innately comprehend what is obvious yet incomprehensible for so many.

The next chapter will show you how to give the gift of yourself *to yourself and to the world* by making a living doing your purpose!

Your Dream Job

CHAPTER FIVE

Your Dream Job

THE GENDER REVEAL for our 2nd child went viral on social media in 2018. It was even featured on a national TV show. We were dumfounded! My wife Yana was simply looking for a way to get me directly involved. Her novel idea was for her girlfriend to secretly blow-dry ultra-fine blue or pink powder into the exhaust pipes of my Lamborghini which would then emit a cloud of pink or blue smoke when I start the engine. I received an influx of direct messages on IG, the majority of which were requests for me to teach 'whatever it was I did for a living to be able to afford a Lamborghini.'

At the peak of these inquiries, my family and I were in China for the first time hiking the Great Wall. Needless to say, I did not hike very far with our 2-year-old son on my back and a three-month pregnant wife! We were brave or nuts for flying so far with a toddler and one in the oven!

I reflected on the 3,000-mile wall that took approximately 2,000 years to construct. I learned that it is also referred to as "The Longest Cemetery" since over one million men died during its construction and were buried along its path because there was no way to transport them back to family for proper burial. Sad. Humbling. Sobering. Life is short, isn't it? We live. We love. We experience. We are inspired. We inspire. We create. We build. And we die. Those that died while building the Great Wall likely had no personal interest or connection to it whatsoever; yet they spent so much of their lives working on it — possibly even dying for it.

As an empath my heart was heavy thinking of the men and their families. I also deeply pondered each person that contacted me for career direction — primarily over a car. The convergence of emotions I felt reflecting on the men and their families whom sacrificed so much for the building of a wall and my own contemporaries being so eager to give of themselves for yet another "thing" was significant. How easily we forget *time* is so much more valuable than *everything* else. It is not about what someone *else* does. What matters most is that we develop the ability to listen internally, piece together our own puzzle and unlock what we ourselves should be doing with our time, energy and gifts.

Life is a journey to your "within." There is no shortage of people seeking to manipulate and exploit others in the name of money or obtaining bigger and better things. Yet deep down no one really wants to be told and scripted. We want to be free… self-aware, driven and empowered; doing what personally moves us, having fun and manifesting the life *we* want to live. Don't get me wrong. Mentorship and learning from each other are good things. However, it cannot be understated:

Everything outside of your being are stimuli or clues prodding you to awaken to what has always been inside of you.

Here is how it works. We subconsciously draw everything we experience. Our experiences are stimuli to help the conscious mind connect to the heart or spirit. For example, I *experienced* the Great Wall and countless social media direct messages at the same time, but it was my decision to tune into my heart that revealed the purpose and what to do next. I felt compelled to channel my heart, the fallen men of the Great Wall and those asking for help into a video message. One of the things that bring me deep inner joy is seeing and where possible, *helping* stimulate others to greater levels of happiness, appreciation and realization of *their* power and purpose.

"AND WHAT DO YOU DO?"

Perhaps you have been asked that question while mingling at a party. Interestingly, *"What do you do?"* is a shallow and paradoxically profound question at the same time. "The full question used to be "What do you do for a living?" Maybe people decided the last part sounded too intrusive or crude, so they dropped it for a measure of decorum.

But there really is no way to make the questioning of what someone does to sustain their life any less crude. Some might argue they ask this not to socially bucket and pigeonhole people, but to learn more about the individual. That would be great, except we all know the unfortunate reality is people rarely earn their living doing something they personally love or experience deep joy doing. Therefore, what someone does for work generally provides little to zero insight into the depth of the individuals character.

Despite the typically shallow intent of the question, what one does for work largely *does* in fact define them because our job is the #1 thing that consumes by far and away the greatest amount of our most valuable asset — time.

There is no denying most humans will spend most of their waking hours working at a job or business. Considering time is infinitely more valuable than money, shouldn't doing what we love for work be infinitely more important than maximizing income potential? Remember the plague of "undeveloped desire?" Another example of undeveloped desire is trading your most valuable asset, for something far less valuable (money), so you can buy *things* that experience has already taught you are even less valuable!

To put it into financial terms, doing something you do not love or enjoy for work is like trading a $100 bill for a $1 bill. Talk about irony! If you choose to *remain* in a career or business ownership you do not sincerely enjoy purely for money you have not heeded your own life lessons. How long will your desire remain undeveloped? How long until you connect the dots?

As alluded to earlier, some may reason "I do something I care nothing about for work because it pays well; and if I make enough money, I will then be able to personally use more of my time!" There are two problems with this. First, the future is not guaranteed, you can pass on at any moment. Secondly, working with the goal of eventually *not* working implicates a life devoid of work is the optimum goal. This mindset is a telltale sign of being in the *wrong* field of work! Work properly aligned with the inner-self is enjoyable, rejuvenating and fulfilling. One way to measure how well your career or business supports your purpose is how the thought of no longer working makes you feel. If no longer working seems so awesome you can't wait to retire then your soul might be prodding you to reevaluate how you are using your most valuable asset.

As we progress through childhood, adolescence, and young adulthood, the things we perceive to make us happy become progressively influenced by external sources like media, television, movies and of course, the disposition of people immediately around us. We begin to prefer money and the illusion of material security over experiences, activities, and endeavors that genuinely feel great. Our authentic essence becomes buried under a litany of learned, artificial, and trite ideals and behavioral patterns which all but eradicate our ability to heed the internal compass. The good news is that if you are reading this book, you are awakening to your power to live intrinsically unbounded and without compulsion.

Before alignment there must be understanding. Remember, the deeper your understanding of what makes *the CEO of your life* tick, the better you can please you. Ready to evaluate yourself on what sort of steward you have been of your most valuable asset?

Face and Save Yourself:

Ask yourself, "Which best describe my circumstances?"

1. What I do for work comes ultra-naturally and I really love it! If this applies to you, congrats! You are among the rare who live in abundance. **Your Grade: A+**

2. I do not love what I do but I also do not hate it, and the work at least utilizes some of my key attributes and talents. If this applies to you, you are close to the abundance of fully maximizing your time. **Your Grade: C-**

3. I simply hate what I do for work. **Your Grade: F**

If the statement you most closely identify with is an "F" don't get down on yourself or panic. It is just as easy to get to an "A" from an "F" as it is from a "C." The first step is to begin placing higher priority on feeling joy and lower priority on the monetary result. Take a breath, I did not say immediately quit your day job to pursue your hobby! I said begin placing a higher priority. Just shifting your attention and energy to this awareness will cause many small things to happen organically.

Imagine the following playing out for you. You begin *spending* less money on things because you are busier *doing* things that you love. Since you are doing more of what you love, your vibrational frequency elevates which increases your creativity. With a desire to engage your passion even more coupled with a *reduced* emphasis on *"things"* you identify ways to downsize your financial obligations so you can spend yet more time doing what you love.

Your expenses are now lower than ever, and you have fewer things, yet oddly you are somehow happier than you have been in a long time! You notice that you are feeling lighter, nimbler and with additional clarity of thought resulting in even more creativity which is now flowing off the charts. New ideas to monetize your passion are flooding in. These ideas combined with your light-hearted positivity and ability to live on less causes you to notice an opportunity to reduce your full-time job hours to part-time hours. The old "you" would have never spotted this window and would have wondered 'why anyone would ever want to reduce their hours'. You are beginning to emanate the vibrational frequency of someone fully conscious and in control of their time and energy – a proper "Boss." You are comfortably supported, working fewer hours and doing *more* of what you love. Since momentum begets momentum, within 6 months you have matched the part-time income of your former full-time job and have become an entrepreneur!

This organic journey was driven by the heart. We know this because the focus was always on the energy/feeling and none of the answers were known in advance. However, if you are logically wired and need to have a plan and know each step in advance, you will prefer the journey to your purpose be lead practically by the mind.

How might you do this? Since the mind is figuratively younger than the heart which is connected to the spirit or essence that precedes birth, the mind is more susceptible to environmental influence and fear. Hence you must begin by conditioning the mind to resist the strong tendency to revert back to focusing on the extrinsic—money, social accolades, admiration of others, or acceptance. This will be quite challenging – more challenging in fact than being led by the heart. However, with concerted effort to shift your priorities, it will feel as if a soothing thread begins to stitch the internal vision you hold for your life with your reality.

After reading motivational stories of success and entrepreneurship you realize the greatest earning potential of every human comes from doing what they are naturally or *intrinsically* passionate about. This by the way is yet another lesson that life has been teaching you:

The most successful people love what they do so much they do not consider it work.

For the thinker, below is the logical step-by-step formula for identifying fulfilling secular work that aligns with your true purpose.

Step 1: Distill Your Essence

Ask yourself:

- What do those that knew me in my infancy and childhood say were my three most prominent personality traits?

____

____

____

- What are the three things I enjoy doing most?

____

____

____

- What are the top three things I love to talk and read about?

____

____

____

When you ask older family members and childhood friends what you were like as a baby and throughout childhood, you may be amazed and enlightened by what you hear. You might also bust a gut laughing! My personal journey to my purposeful or *joyful* dream job was the organic, heart-based path outlined earlier. However, when I also take the cerebral approach by reflecting on things people have told me about my essence as an infant and toddler, it leads me right to the same place and makes perfect sense. I have hear things like, "You were always staring at people's mouths with intense eyes and squinted eyebrows like you had a super-strong need to understand them." "You were so sensitive." "You were dying to speak." In third or fourth grade, my reading and comprehension scores were collegiate level. In my teens, a close friend so much older than me, I was the ring bearer in his wedding, began facetiously calling me "Aaron the great reasoner" for my ability to see all perspectives and extract lessons and positivity from seemingly any situation or topic.

What careers highly favor listening, speaking,

empathy, problem-solving and the ability to see things from both sides and all angles which is a hallmark of good negotiating? Sales, entrepreneurship, writing, filmmaking, teacher, attorney are all among the careers my authentic essence would excel at! My career evolution has included several of these. Intriguingly, the first two – sales and entrepreneurship, while enjoyable, do not bring enough joy and fulfillment I would do them for free. Based upon the grading scale above, no matter how much I made, if I only created businesses and sold stuff, I would have to give myself a "C" grade. Conversely, connecting with people through writing, speaking and even film comes so naturally and is so fulfilling that I would and have done it for free.

Take the time to do these exercises. Without question, prioritizing and synthesizing what effectively becomes the sketch of your aura and blueprint of your purpose – that thing you should be spending most of your time on this earth doing – will emerge. If you want to enrichen the journey to your within, ask *"why?" and "how long have I been this way?"* after each of your answers to unlock progressively deeper truths about who and what you really are.

Step 2: Industry and Job Alignment

Next you analyze jobs that heavily leverage aspects of your essence derived from Step 1. This is the only time data might come into play because figuring out what you should do should not be overly data driven. Your purpose is not something that requires a roadmap from others; you are not them… their journey is not your journey. After making a list of jobs and businesses that strongly favor your gifts, aptitudes, interests, and passions, one or two will emerge and energetically draw you more than the others.

Step 3: Identify How Your Job or Business Will Help Others

In a world that places so much emphasis on money, status or even just making ends meet one of the most important aspects of our purpose is often lost. *Nurturing and serving others.*

A lesson of how critical the need to nurture each other is to our purpose is once again taught by children. Just observe toddlers at play, undoubtedly one child will take a toy for themselves, unwilling to share it causing another child to cry. In this behavior we observe the fundamental necessity of satisfying oneself. There is nothing wrong with this. On an airplane we are instructed to first put the mask on ourselves likely to avoid fainting trying to help another person and *both* dying. Similarly, we must love ourselves before we can truly love another person.

When you explain to the child who took the toy their behavior hurt the other child causing them to cry; and *empower* them with the ability to help make them feel better something interesting often happens. The disposition of the perpetrating child transforms into the most nurturing, comforting and consoling energy. They are then willing to share *any* toy that might help their friend feel better. As the crying child positively responds to their gesture, the joy and higher vibrational energy of the perpetrating child is easily evident. They clearly enjoy their power to nurture and do good more than taking and having the toy all to themselves.

Be careful *not* to ignore this aspect of your purpose. Jot down a list of the many ways doing what you love most — which will become your job or business — can also serve, elevate or enhance the experience of others. Ironically, besides experiencing more intrinsic joy, more money also results! We will discuss this in greater detail in chapter 6.

____

____

____

Step 4: Be Complete

All human knowledge regarding energy, across science and ancient books of wisdom and religion, confirm that for energy – both literal and figurative (faith)– to be conducted, the circuit must be complete. We are energy. When we commit to things that authentically move the heart we become "complete," undivided, less impacted by interference and our purpose is conducted. If we work on a job we hate, the resulting level of satisfaction is obviously very low with finite and low income. If we are doing what we moderately like while secretly wishing we were doing something different which we deeply love, we can expect our ongoing fulfillment to be commensurately moderate with relatively modest and with finite income potential.

People often refer to those who make a lot of money doing what they love as "lucky". They have a dream job and are rich! What everyone fails to realize is that the thing that has enabled these people to live a dream is less about luck and more about a single choice that all of us can make. That choice is a *commitment* to do what you love most as your secular work and primary source of income. It is really that simple. If the idea that anyone can have a dream job complete with high income sounds unrealistic remember Newton's third law that states 'every force has an equal and opposite reaction.'

Considering them "lucky" not only discounts

their hard work and proficiency, but also completely overlooks the fact that these individuals quite typically *worked for free* at some point along their journey – including yours truly! Do you see the parallel with Newton's third law? Working for free and even enduring poverty seems extreme. The equal and opposite reaction to extreme poverty and perhaps darkness of occasionally loosing hope is becoming rich doing what one loves and being full of light and joy. Semi-pro sports pay little to nothing. Racecar drivers and motorcycle racers and their parents spend thousands if not hundreds of thousands before ever generating income. Artists such as singers, actors, writers and comedians may work hundreds of jobs for little to no pay for years before their proverbial break. Entrepreneurs not only work for free but leverage personal assets such as their home to realize their purpose.

While the seemingly impossible securing of a "dream job" is not so impossible, it is in fact rare. However, it is not rare for the serendipitous reasons. What makes having a dream job so rare is that it is the result of a person being intrinsically-driven, possessive of deep heart connection, alignment with purpose, joy and unwavering belief. I will never blindly mentor someone that is primarily seeking money and other extrinsic outcomes. I will also never hire someone that just wants the job but have no passion or joy in the work. To do so is to assist them in squandering their most valuable asset (time) and the satisfaction of doing work in alignment with their greater purpose. It is the moral responsibility of leaders to not only inspire others to follow *their* direction, but to follow their own heart first.

If you want to live your dream job continue looking within and heeding the lessons your soul is trying to teach you. Commit to making your purpose of experiencing joy and maximum intrinsic fulfillment top priority and see how the quality of your life improves.

Empathy Can
Make You Millions

Empathy Can Make You Millions

ONE DAY WHILE working from a coffee shop, I observed a new acquaintance whom was apparently a regular buzzing around the shop speaking to people. Everyone that greeted her gave her the biggest deepest hug you had ever seen. It was like they were looking into her soul and they loved her. I sat there in amazement as this happened repeatedly and I thought to myself: "She would be great at sales." When I mentioned this, her immediate response was: "Oh no, I could never do sales."

A couple of weeks later I was having a drink with a successful filmmaker. Discussing how he maintains a steady flow of projects; he exclaims that he too 'could never do sales.' I thought "What is with this? Why are people so quick to assert they could never do sales?" There are all sorts of untrue and derogatory pop culture myths about what it takes to succeed in sales and in business. One misconception is that you must be overly ambitious and money hungry. Another is that to achieve great success you must be selfish, perhaps unscrupulous and willing to do whatever it takes to close the deal or get ahead — pretty much be an ass. *I am living proof that nice guys and girls finish first!*

I have earned millions of dollars selling transformative business software and services to some of the largest and most complex corporations in the world. Consistently defying odds and achieving unprecedented outcomes, I attribute my success to two core principles which apply to nearly all professions and industries including pharmaceuticals, financial services, manufacturing, retail, construction, entertainment and music, oil and gas, real estate, etc. These two simple principles are not rocket science— in fact, we all naturally practice them every day!

EMPATHY AND INTERSECTIONS

Whether you are the CEO of a medium to large corporation, the receptionist, whether you sell electronics, used cars, houses or financial services, your success hinges on these two things: *empathy* and *intersections*. How so? Take the CEO of a large corporation.

If I am the CEO of a large corporation I care

about the experience of my employees, I care about meeting and exceeding the financial performance my Board of Directors and shareholders expect for the company, I care about the high-quality product and experience my customers expect, and I have my vision of how I would like to see the company evolve to perform even better. As the CEO, my efficacy and ultimate success depend upon my ability to find the point(s) where all these agendas intersect —where everyone's objectives are met — then skillfully balance and linger at these intersections to drive peak performance. Lingering at the intersections means listening, confirming, re-confirming and communicating the direct benefits to each respective constituency naturally and organically.

The better the CEO the higher the quality of the intersections and the more diligently the team works and come together in support of corporate direction; feeling heard and confident their interests are served in parallel. On the other hand, breakdowns in product quality, sales performance, employee satisfaction or customer satisfaction often indicate a CEO that is perceived as disingenuous and untrustworthy – lacking in empathy – or ineffective at lingering and operationalizing intersections.

What about a receptionist? As the receptionist the information you have will help any visitor that comes to the business. You know where everyone sits in the company, their contact information and other pertinent information such as roles and responsibilities, events and schedules. There might be a rapid fire and high-volume flow of visitors and phone calls requiring you to be ultra-efficient. Customers want to feel valued and unrushed. When they call or visit, you skillfully listen and then efficiently direct them accordingly. If you do it well enough you help create a better experience for customers and reputation for the company as well as yourself by not allowing phone calls or visitors to queue up.

Moving away from business and imagine you are at a cocktail party. As you mingle, you are cognizant that people are seeking to have intriguing and stimulating conversations. They are eager to listen, but they also want to talk about themselves. You naturally seek to strike a balance between talking about yourself while drawing them out and actively listening. You empathetically found and lingered at the intersection of both of your needs. After each conversation, you intuitively know how well you did – did you talk too much or not enough?

If that made you think "no duh!", it should have! Empathy and intersections come 100% naturally and are foundational to our purpose as human beings. We possess a healthy need to serve ourselves; balanced with a need to nurture and serve others. In this way, no matter the context business success comes down to these two things.

If you are especially empathic, you have an

advantage at being great at sales and business. Your life experiences have repeatedly provided evidence, you just have not noted the lesson. So, reflect. Have not your most pleasurable experiences with sales-people been with ones that do *not* seem like they only care about themselves and selling you? You could feel when their energy and motives were fueled by a sincere desire to help and add value to whatever need or challenge you faced.

There is an endless array of books and training programs designed to help people sell more by implementing some of the *behavioral* traits of empathy. However, those who possess empathy as a hallmark trait will naturally have an advantage — pun intended. Bottom line... Nice guys and girls do *not* finish last. If you are empathic you have the foundation of a high-performing superstar sales-person and leader. Most agree there are too many of the purely money and ego-driven types in sales and general leadership. If this were not the case salespeople and bosses would not have such a bad name! Imagine the value you could, therefore, bring yourself and the world with a rewarding career in sales and leadership.

SALES IS LEADERSHIP SQUARED

One of the simplest definitions of leadership is, "the art of motivating a group of people to act towards achieving a common goal." This happens to also be a precise definition of the "art" of selling! Clients do not award the order or sale due to force but through positive internal motivation. Interestingly, while it is often assumed that general leadership is more complex, exacting more skill or experience than sales, they are not only similar, but sales can actually be more complex and require greater skill and dexterity than executive leadership!

I was 23 years old when I landed my first high-income business transformation sales job. By high income, I mean a six-figure base salary with total income being several hundred thousand dollars depending on performance. My territory consisted of several named accounts across the western half of North America including Alaska and Canada. I was by far the youngest and least educated on a team of expert sales executives averaging 15-20 years my senior. Our product was both expensive and complex mission-critical OSS (Operational Support System) software for hi-speed data and phone communications service providers. The term mission-critical means if the software fails the company's ability to make money would be lost or severely impaired. The converse is also true – namely when our software works as designed the business would capture greater market share and generate more revenue. To whom within a company would you say those objectives are most important? You guessed it, the CEO. Also, the Chief Operating Officer (COO), Chief Financial Officer (CFO) and other members of the senior executive team.

The software automated operations across multiple departments. How cohesive and streamlined operations and departments performed could be the single determining factor in whether these executives of emerging telecommunications companies got to retire early due to a successful IPO or being acquired by a larger company. I had to earn enough *trust* and *respect* of executives who often had children older than me, for them to become motivated to follow my lead and invest $2-$6 million dollars with the expectation we would help them achieve their fiscal goals.

Sound daunting? This is just the beginning! Telecommunications was just the *first* industry I sold multi-million-dollar business transformation software to. Throughout my 20-year career, I sold to and enabled Fortune 500 Retail, Manufacturing, Travel, Banking, Insurance and Healthcare to adopt or improve e-commerce, sell and service through multiple channels, measure and improve digital customer experience, enterprise marketing, procurement efficiency, streamline patient care as well as manufacturing, logistics and supply-chain operations.

All of the systems I sold introduced significant organizational change to hundreds and sometimes thousands of employees. It is no secret humans notoriously hate change. Human resistance to change is so great that one of the CEO's core responsibilities is to *prepare* the people of his organization for change. The CEO and other senior executives daily observe the condition of the seas ahead and methodically implement changes to keep the business afloat and thriving. Middle management often *begrudgingly* cascade said changes to their subordinates expecting backlash. Employees often remain in a state of perpetual fight or flight as they await what they consider to be the 'next unwelcome change.' Such are the energies I have observed working closely with all levels of hundreds of corporation cultures.

If I succeed in earning the respect of key executives including the CEO that our platform will deliver a strong Return on Investment (ROI), another curve is thrown. Partly to ensure the users love what is selected, and partly to avert exclusive accountability for a failed multi-million-dollar investment, the CEO or lead executive would often defer final vendor selection to the employees. I must lead and inspire people often pre-wired to hate change and sometimes threatened by the very automation my software brings — to become positive about change and personally select me as their partner instead of four or five of my biggest competitors.

Remember what we discussed earlier about how people often have unpleasant experiences with salespeople? Selling products and services that will impact the day-to-day lives of thousands of employees is a lot like running for office. Politicians also have a bad reputation! Also similar to running for office you do not get to just schmooze the "big shots" and call it a day. You must take genuine personal interest in the people, walk in their shoes and identify ways to help them on *their* terms.

In addition to navigating the fears, resistance to change, negative preconceived ideas about salespeople and individual egos within my *clients*, I must also do the same within my own company! At an enterprise technology company, a bevy of brilliant engineers, product managers, implementation consultants and even the CEO and senior executive team follow the leadership of the field sales executive. I have to be the catalyst of transmuting challenging and conflicting energies of my co-workers into trust, motivation and cohesion around two objectives: delivering value to our clients with genuine empathy while maximizing revenue and return on our assets.

As challenging as my career was, it was a great commercial fit for me because I was able to significantly exercise and capitalize on one of my strongest traits –*Empathy*. Being empathic imbues one with an innate ability to sense the emotional energetic disposition of nearly everyone they come into contact with. When you genuinely want to help and have the capacity plus proficiency to do so, you become trusted. Without trust, there is no chance of securing business.

Empathic or not, it is impossible for any salesperson or leader to be liked by everyone. This is especially so if your appearance is different than people they are accustomed to being led by. This is a lesson that even leaders with the best intentions must learn and sometimes painfully come to terms with. *You are simply not going to be appreciated by everyone.* I once had one of my exotic cars keyed in the parking lot of a company I consistently over-performed for. I was 24 or 25. Although it was painful to experience it also taught me firsthand that others can possess just as much negative energy without reason as I possess positive. The experience helped me learn the importance of not allowing external events to alter my internal disposition and desire to do good for myself and for others.

Whether leadership through sales or general executive leadership the objective is the same — to assist and motivate what might be some of the most varied and complex entities in the universe — human beings. As a business transformation sales executive, at any given point, I was leading 7-10 different multi-million-dollar opportunities per year. Remember, enterprise software is business transformative because it typically affects and introduces change to multiple departments of a business substantially improving business outcomes. That means, in contrast to pure executive leadership where said leaders are challenged to effectively lead within their single organizational culture; the business sales executive learns to rapidly intuitively comprehend, adapt and effectively lead and motivate within *hundreds* of organizational cultures throughout their career! For this reason, I jokingly say a tenure in this type of career should be calculated in dog years! An executive with 10 years of experience leading within the respective companies they work for has just that — 10 years of experience.

Meanwhile, the business sales executive with the same 10 years has 10 years with their own company *plus* an average of perhaps 7-10 different client organizations in which they might lead multi-faceted sales campaigns each year. That is a total of 70-100 years of observing and leading within disparate varied and unique corporate cultures. With the distinctive vantage point of serving as partner to all levels from senior executive to staff worker of hundreds of major companies, I collected encyclopedia volumes of observations and insight. Procedural governance that works or does not. Things that inspire and motivate as well as what torpedo morale and cohesion. Leadership archetypes that do or do not fit various cultures and situations. In fact, it is this insight that has helped me to as needed leverage specific members from my own various executive teams at the precise time and in a precise way to close tens of millions of dollars.

Whether sales or general leadership, never forget leadership is the business of people. It is unfortunate that the strongest motive of many who want to lead is typically appearances, money or both. Can either of these deliver much less sustain genuine fulfillment? As common as it is to experience bad salespeople, bad bosses are even more universally experienced! Similar to bad salespeople, many seek positions of authority for the same reasons as bad salespeople — ego and money.

Then there are those leaders that have an unmistakable quality. It is as if they see each of their subordinates as sleeping giants under their *temporary stewardship*.

The best leaders know each subordinate has the potential to surpass even them!

Have you ever experienced such leadership? If so, you likely felt dignified, respected and valued. You believed and *knew* they had your best interest at heart; which moved you to follow their lead and work even harder.

The thing that enables the best leaders to see and believe in your unlimited potential is derived from *empathy*. Nothing in their mind is fixed about *you* because nothing in their mind is fixed about *themselves!* Intrinsically aware of a time when they too were sleeping giants – unaware of their purpose – the greatest leaders never stop expanding; they never believe they have 'arrived.' Their quintessential growth mindset also fuels their greatness.

"Nice guys finish last." "Look out for number 1." "Winning isn't everything, it's the only thing." These popular quotes which are often used to motivate sales and business leaders contradict empathetic concern for others. To live by them is to defy our nature, purpose and the undeniable fact that empathy is foundational not only to good business but all human relationships. Instead of brushing empathy aside like a pesky sign of weakness to be suppressed, seek to cultivate it. For empathy can make you millions!

PART THREE

Love & Relationships

Tired of Bad Relationships…
Do This!

CHAPTER SEVEN

Tired of Bad Relationships… Do This!

WE ALL WANT… check that… we all *need* love. We need family or tribe, friends and also romantic love. But why does it seem conflict and deep pain always seem to accompany love? Why is compatible and enduring romantic love so elusive?

Everything we have discussed has been about becoming more intrinsically aware, empowered and accountable for the results and experiences of our life. Romantic love, while one of the most important human necessities, is also one of the things in life we least understand. The result is that it has become the norm to project accountability for why one has not yet found compatible and fulfilling romantic partnerships everywhere but internally. "There are no good single men!" "Women are psycho nowadays." "Men are dogs." "Men are immature."

Remember, *you* are the top steward and CEO of your life; making your experience in each area of your life the direct result of the quality of *your* stewardship. As with everything else in life, the source of all our success *and* our challenges lie within. All challenged or 'failed' relationships whether platonic friendships, familial, or romantic have the same macro forensics — temporary or perpetual lack of energetic vibrational alignment. Consciously going within to better understand the subconscious energy you embody, will allow you to observe and understand your relationships — or lack thereof — through a lens of objectivity and insight that is anchored by your own internal truth instead of learned binders like ego and fear.

Let's begin our introspective analysis of romantic love from the top. What typically happens when one goes on a date or meets someone for the first time and there is romantic intent to find a life partner? The occasion often feels more like a meeting of two businesspeople or dignitaries! Each person's respective "ambassador" gets thrust front and center as two painstakingly curated facades engage in the ritualistic verbal dance of getting to know each other. The ego-mind objective of each performance is to be as appealing as possible to the other person. The infinitely wiser heart or spirit has the objective of simply ascertaining whether there exists enough effortless compatibility and synergy to last a lifetime.

Can you see the disconnect already? Next thing you know we are completely focused on "showcasing" ourselves with little to zero regard for whether our display is a whole and realistic depiction of ourselves; much less whether the other person's flatteringly positive responses to our ambassadorship are even genuine! There are only two situations seeking to impress the other person might deliver the desired outcome – fantasy role-play or dating purely for "fun." However, when trying to find a special match, the proverbial armchair partner or soulmate *this is not the time for ambassadorship*.

One definition of compatibility is 'a state in which two things are able to exist or occur together without problems or conflict.' When it comes to deciding whom to spend the rest of our life with, we should add something to the end of that definition. Compatibility — "a state in which two things are able to exist or occur together without problems or conflict — *without extensive or significant alteration to either party!*" If you do not expand your comprehension of what it means to be truly compatible, you will find yourself repeatedly falling in love with *ambassadors* — altered and curated versions of your love interests — only to realize you are completely incompatible with the actual person!

Since one cannot give what they do not have and like attracts like; a healthy understanding and appreciation of oneself, also known as "self-love," must exist before one can give or receive such from another. After all, how can a person expect to be loved if external "binders" impair the comprehension of their true essence and ability to unconditionally love themselves? The overarching theme of this book is becoming aware of binders and how our behavioral patterns are *supporting* or *undermining* the realization of your purpose of joy and fulfillment.

If you are looking for a life partner or a more aligned relationship, here is a contemplative, empowering yet fun activity you can immediately begin incorporating into your dating.

Aaron's List Swap

Create a list of traits you desire in a mate — from must-have requirements right down to things that seem like small preferences. All manner of topics or categories should be covered. Be sure to include even very specific and nice-to-have items like, "he or she will be a morning person, a night owl, laugh at my corny jokes, will *want* to massage my feet, be spontaneous, randomly affectionate, enjoy giving and receiving non sexual affection, have high sex drive, have low sex drive, enjoy going to sporting events," etc. This is your chance to be completely focused on you! Visualize and create day-to-day scenarios of life in your head then notate even scenario-based traits of the most ideal partner for you.

WHAT I DESIRE IN A MATE?

Now it gets really interesting. Ask your prospective partner to create a similar list and the two of you swap lists and evaluate yourselves against the *other* person's requirements! Transparently look at each preference and requirement noting the degree to which each item is an easy natural fit for you or not so much. Evaluating yourselves against the other person's list is very different than the typical implementation of a list whereby one silently tries to measure the other person against written preferences. The challenge with this approach is that the results are based upon what *we* believe – *or want to believe* – to be true about them. We are unable to effectively spot incompatibility because the other person's ambassador is center stage at the beginning.

When we introspectively evaluate *ourselves,* we are less likely to project our ambassador into the equation. Why? How successful have you been at breaking bad habits? Starting good new habits? Losing weight? Considering how hard it is to change for *ourselves,* we have virtually no chance of changing for another person. Knowing in advance the needs and desires of the other person allows us to either enter with eyes wide open or avert heartache before it begins. There is no good reason to enter a relationship with someone you know in advance that you will be hard pressed to satisfy.

It is critical to do the list swap within the first day or two as soon as there are signs of mutual chemistry but *before* getting too emotionally invested — after which objectivity basically goes out the window. If you wait too long, the natural need to belong and feel loved can be so strong that we will unconsciously fight to ensure the new relationship does not fail even if it actually needs to fail fast. Before you know it, you have sugarcoated and watered-down pills of incompatibility that will absolutely come back to haunt you later. Also, the sooner the list swap is done the harder it is for either to misleadingly add items to their list to fake compatibility based upon what they may have already learned about the other person.

Thought the list swap is not foolproof it can save you time and energy while increasing the odds of forging a happy, balanced naturally compatible and fulfilling relationship!

The Elephant in the Room… Sex

CHAPTER EIGHT

The Elephant in the Room… Sex

AFTER DETERMINING THERE is chemistry and compatibility eventually comes another decision. When to have sex. Sexuality has such a huge presence not just for those dating but in marriages as well. Sex is not only super fun and instinctive for the continuance of our species, it also spans the physical, psychological and emotional, making it one of the most powerful underlying forces at work within us. Even without a conscious goal of sexual intercourse, sex drive is the ever-present subconscious motivator of everything from how we dress and groom to how we comport ourselves in social settings and even in business. We are constantly proving our worthiness to both the opposite and even the same sex. Obviously, when dating sex is naturally anything but subconscious.

While sexual desire is natural, I am amazed at

how *unnaturally* it is often managed. Both men and women are guilty of mismanaging their sexual desire to their own detriment. Men tend to focus too much on physical neglecting the emotional and spiritual aspects of intimacy. Women are often so fearful of being marginalized and primarily valued for sex they create a different set of psychological challenges for themselves. "When should I have sex?" While all women do not struggle with this question, many do. My mother-in-law who found herself dating again in her mid-50s even grappled with this.

Whether or not this is a personal challenge for you, it is worth using your imagination and working through this dilemma to practice going within to arrive at your own personal truth. Purely for the sake of simplicity, we will speak in the context of a hetero-sexual woman, but men and those who identify as LGBT wrestle with this issue as well.

We all have heard from friends or seen movies and television shows that feature women struggling with "when" they should have sex with someone they are dating. A popular TV personality —in effort to help women —may have inadvertently exacerbated the issue by advising that women should not 'give up sex' for at least 90 days to increase the odds that the man stays around longer and perhaps even marries her. Considering we have been discussing the power, freedom and joy that results from living intrinsically — instead of being overly influenced by ideals and things extrinsic to our being — can you already detect the misalignment?

There are several issues with ascribing an artificial timeframe as well as the idea that sex is 'given up.' Let's first consider how the idea of 'giving up sex' has a negative connotation implicating a surrendering or giving something to the other person. If one is truly internally anchored, not seeking to control the feelings of another person or inordinately in need to assimilate to external ideals and labels they would not even do it after 90 days if they don't want to! Conversely, if they are ready by day five, they would be fine doing it then as well. Some women either forget about their own sexuality or for some reason perpetuate a narrative they are only giving not receiving and enjoying for themselves.

Even one of the most successful female vocalists in history and a powerful advocate of personal power said in a song something to the effect of: 'She has needs too. After sex is all over, he can leave.'

The point is not promiscuity, it is about embodying one's *own* power within. Throughout this book, we are reminded to get to the root of any challenge or anxiety by going within to assess whether our behavior is working for or against our purpose of joy. Here, a woman is concerned she might be considered 'loose' or deemed untrust-worthy and not marriage material. The other fear is that if a man is 'given' sex too soon, he may not stick around as long or value her. The ultimate question is whether these ideals and supposedly cautionary behavior are *helping* or possibly *hindering* her purpose of experiencing joy and attracting a connection that grows into a life-long aligned and happy partnership.

If this is something you have struggled with, consider a couple of points. If he attracted you, he is probably also attractive to other women. It is estimated that men have about 10 times the sex drive as a woman. To put that into perspective:

If a woman thinks about sex twice per day a man has thought about it 20 times!

What are the odds an otherwise healthy man goes 90 days without sex? A woman that meets a man and has some idea that she is going to immediately alter his personal pattern and physical needs due to her forcibly putting him on sex probation might be unconsciously encouraging the very thing she fears most... him having sex with other women on her watch! Since you just met, it is unlikely he will feel the need to make any significant changes and be monogamous so soon.

I suppose if one insisted on trying to control and manipulate how someone else will value them, they could strategize and plan to 'give up sex' somewhere after the third date and before his initial infatuation is overpowered by nature and his pre-existing pattern of having casual sex with other women. The only problem is that there is no way to know where that tipping point is. Plus, the very nature of your concern conspires against your objectives in several other ways. Sex is one of the most basic instincts of humans and even animals and is also universally available. By anxiously worrying he may vanish or no longer desire a relationship after having sex with you, it is actually *you* who has made sex the most valuable thing you have to offer — inadvertently marginalizing *yourself*. The notion that sex is anyone's *unique* value or some elixir that if taken at the precise time will grant a longer-lasting and fulfilling partnership is another illusionary "binder."

Binders gain increasing control over us because they are self-fulfilling. The fear of being undervalued or *only* valued for sex portrays a strong belief there is a *lack* of quality suitors. Now go within. Has life not taught you that you attract what you expect or believe to be true? Our experiences reflect what we believe. On this basis, it could be said that this fear-based disposition actually introduces risk rather than averting it! Placing so much emphasis on sex as if it were the hinge pin for your love could cause additional challenges later in the relationship or marriage when you go through a period of low sex drive or experience mutual complacency. The adage, "live by the sword, die by the sword" comes to mind.

Men and women are peers. Yes, they are physiologically different, but they are partners in life. Neither should feel like they are surrendering or giving something up. If you hold the disposition of having to "give up" something in expectation of love, then a weaker unempowered partner is what you will embody in the relationship. Lastly and somewhat humorously, by viewing sex as a 'treat he earns', she not only marginalizes herself but is already treating him like a dog. Careful what you start!

Contrary to the implications of this fear-based binder, both men and women value each other for more than sex. This is especially true of those seeking a deeper than physical connection. For those that are only seeking sex, the last thing you want to do is manipulate them in a way that causes them to prematurely change. Life has already proven that humans cannot change other humans. If you are the thing that supposedly 'changed the playboy' you could have a timebomb that explodes when he reverts to his original way and then changes later when *he* is ready.

The love *connection* we all desire is not manufactured or engineered through gamesmanship and strategy. Our ultimate purpose is joy and fulfillment. At the outset of this book we were reminded that our purpose of joy and fulfillment predates things the ego or human mind learns. For this reason, romantic love, perhaps more so than just about any other area of life should not be overly led by the mind. There is a reason love is symbolized by the heart. Evidence you are leaning on your mind too much is *thinking* things like 'I have to prove myself,' 'I cannot call him or her too soon,' 'I must show who's in charge,' and similar thoughts. These fears are rooted in societal ideals where the blind leads the blind further and further away from authenticity and personal power.

When seeking to manipulate other people's views of us we are outside of our own power and have greater exposure to disappointment and heartache.

As mentioned earlier in this chapter, this is not at all about being promiscuous. I would never encourage my daughter to be promiscuous. When she has grown up, we will openly discuss the physical and emotional pros and the potential cons of having sex. As with every other topic in life, I will remind her it is ultimately her truth and ability to remain attuned with a clear connection to her heart and purpose that will determine any cons she experiences and to what degree. And that really is the point!

Should You Stay
or Should You Go

CHAPTER NINE

Should You Stay
or Should You Go

IN CHAPTER 7 we talked about how easy it is to fool oneself into looking past grave incompatibilities of a new romantic acquaintance for fear of losing the connection. The longer we are in a relationship this risk increases. A friend of mine we will call Jackie, was about 37 years old, very attractive, fit and with a successful career to boot. She had been in a committed relationship for about three years and was wondering why he had not yet proposed. I took her through some exercises whereby she would introspectively journey to her within and answer a few questions. The first simple question I instructed her to ask *herself* is: "Do I actually believe he is the one?" I was trying to get her to connect with her inner truth. Was he someone *she* wanted to marry because she could really see herself happy with him forever or was she just seeking an outcome? She turned within and asked herself the question, then quietly pondered. A few moments later she broke the silence and said assertively, "NO he is not!" He was verbally abusive and emotionally unavailable. If she knew in her heart they were incompatible — and was even quite unhappy with him —why on earth did she attach so much expectation and significance to whether he proposed?

If not careful, the desire for "the goal" can be so strong that we lose sight of the experience we seek in accomplishing the goal!

There is all manner of reasons we might continue in a relationship that we know deep down is not a fit —all of them lead back to a fear of some sort. Fear of being alone, fear of failure, fear of being looked at funny due to being single at a certain age, fear of having to do the work of dating again, fear of rejection, on and on. Meanwhile, during the time a person is paired up with the wrong partner, they energetically block the possibility of attracting a more compatible one. You try to make the unduly challenging situation work for years or even decades. Which do you think is better — to be single and shopping or to be married to the wrong person? Fortunately, Jackie heeded her own lesson and exited the relationship. The decision and steps she took were not easy. However, it is the darkest just before the dawn. Within a few months, she met the man that would become her life partner.

The two are aligned in their *purpose* to serve others, are married and have started a family together.

Madison was a pretty 33-year-old woman with an adorable three-year-old daughter. She was fit, warm and fun-loving. I had wondered why it seemed she hadn't had a boyfriend in the 5-6 years I had known her. One day, to my surprise she mentioned she would be bringing a date to our holiday party. "Is he your new boo?" I teased. "No, not really. It's not like that… well, I mean it *could* be…." She managed to say so much and yet so little! She then spills the beans. Apparently, they had been really good *friends* for about three years. The sort of 'really good friends' that he would escort her to holiday parties and special occasions. "So, you guys have never gotten romantic, ever? Do you want to date him?" I asked. Her reply was something to the effect of: 'I have feelings for him, but I don't want it to get awkward and I don't want to pursue him… but I think he kinda feels something too.'

Madison then asked me to broach the subject with her friend in a group conversation including her and see if his intentions might come out. Sure enough, his intentions were suitably unclear. He perfectly straddled the fence leaving possibility open while propping himself up with several weak excuses for why now might not be a good time for a relationship. Madison had been hoping for nearly three years that their relationship would move to the next level! In this case, Madison was stuck with the wrong person without even being with them. She finally acknowledged that he was never assertive enough and deep down she knew he was simply not the right guy for her. Happily, a few months later she was introduced and began dating someone that was much more compatible.

Have you ever been stuck, suspended in fear of facing what you already knew within? Whether we are stuck or progressive it is always an inside job — even when we think other people might be the reason. When you look back on your life in the times you felt stuck are you now able to discern what was really holding you back? Whenever you feel stuck the cause is *always* some form of fear. We already have the answer, but we don't want to face it. We are essentially running from ourselves in protest.

Since we are energetic beings there is only so much we can ignore or run from internal prodding before other aspects of our life feel the repercussions and also become halted. There is no getting around the fact that accessing the courage to heed the direction within is the antidote to becoming "unstuck." Courage is required because instinctive self-preservation wants to avoid change or any pain we might experience or supposedly subject another due to living our truth.

Although fear is extremely low vibe it often masquerades as higher vibrational emotions like love.

Have you ever been in an incompatible relationship yet no matter how imbalanced or challenging it was you found yourself unable to exit because you were morbidly afraid of "breaking their heart?" Even filled with love and empathy and seeking to do good we can be guilty of inadvertently acting from a place of ego. Ego not in the sense of conscious pride but the inflated view we are a necessity to the fulfillment and happiness of another.

Every person is divinely powerful and must find their own truth and optimal expression, including you! To remain in an imbalanced relationship out of compulsion and guilt is a disservice to both effectively bringing down two for the price of one. Neither will fulfill their purpose of joy in this situation. The good news, bad news is that if your energy tells you separation or severance of a relationship is needed, the other person is quite likely equally challenged, scared and stuck.

As always, we find our authentic truth by going within. In contemplating this dilemma, two important lessons life has already taught us come to mind:

1. Love does not require compatibility. Are there not plenty of people whom you love but could never be roommates much less life partners with?

2. Our decision to build a relationship was driven

by our ultimate purpose — joy and fulfillment. Being in a compatible partnership *increases* joy. Being in a highly incompatible partnership *decreases* joy. Self-administered condemnation or ideals that impede your inner joy are externally absorbed binders.

A person's environment may have conditioned them to believe that ending a relationship that is no longer in vibrational alignment makes them a failure or even worse declares them as having poor morals should they divorce. Failure is only *determined* by you since you are the only one that experiences your life! Therefore, the real failure or low moral character is allowing yourself — and the other person — to remain in a state of perpetual stress, conflict and unhappiness.

This applies even when there are children involved. Some have reasoned with good intention: 'I will suffer it out for the kids.' Once again, a person should go within to ascertain whether this course aligns with the purpose of joy they hold for both themselves and for their children. When parents remain unhappily married there are several fears at the root: fear of no longer matching a societal ideal of what it means to be a family i.e. the supposed stigma of a 'broken home,' fear of losing the approval of others, fear that the children will somehow be deprived of a happy childhood.

However, what gradually happens to a person who remains in a marriage that is so misaligned that divorce is being considered? They become so weighed down with anxiety that their true essence is generally nowhere to be found. Close friends of theirs can attest to the person's light and original essence leaving or changing. In a highly unhappy marriage, both parents are thus partial versions of their fullest happy, positive and creative selves. They are lacking in self-love which is in turn felt by the children. Not only do *we* want to be our fullest self, but our *children* also prefer to have 100% of both of their parents.

When a marriage is so vibrationally misaligned that divorce is needed, it is divorce that also delivers *complete* parents back to the children. That a parent would even consider remaining unhappy for their children is a testament of deep parental love. Such parents most certainly have it within them to be present and collaborative co-parents. If unconditional love required compatibility it wouldn't be unconditional. In this way when parents' divorce with genuine love and support for each other, everyone moves closer to realizing their purpose of joy and fulfillment — parents and children are relieved from depleting friction and enjoy having the happier, more aligned full expression of each of their parents.

No one starts a relationship or marriage expecting a breakup or divorce. However, when our soul deems it necessary, surrendering to our inner truth will ultimately benefit everyone involved because we are all connected. Growth is not always pleasant, but it is progressive and has a purpose. As with every other decision, whether or not it is time to divorce should not be extrinsically derived from friends, therapists, pastors or books; but revealed through a strong and clear connection to the heart, spirit and purpose.

You Were Not Dumped!

CHAPTER TEN

You Were Not Dumped!

Now that we have covered how energy works and that nothing, we experience really escapes soul-level awareness, I have to call you out. We have all been there. Those whom this *currently* applies to know who they are. Here is your proverbial shot in the arm. This chapter is intentionally short because it is tough love and because this is something we secretly know but decide to throw a pity party anyway. The narrative you have told yourself and perhaps others — that you were dumped and completely blindsided when 'she ran off with another man' or 'he ran off with another woman' is a lie! In matters of energetic connection — which relationships are — we are *never* blindsided. We always know. Scientifically, energy has to shake hands with the other side — that is conduction.

Similarly, without awareness and cooperation of both sides, there could never be a connection. Just as you absolutely know when someone holding your hand lets go, we intuitively sense the quality of a relationship or connection real-time with and without words. That means we knew the relationship was in trouble long before any outward act or severance by the other person. The issue is that we chose to ignore and run from the problem essentially running from ourselves — acknowledgement of our fears.

Since childhood, we have been trying to have our cake and eat it too. As children, we could not wait to grow up and become powerful and strong. At the same time, we also loved being the consummate victim — eager to be pitied by Mom, Dad and anyone that would listen. As we grow up, we learn it is not such a good look or experience to be pitied. However, occasionally we relapse. Love is one of those areas we love to relapse.

Eager to be the victim, we fail to acknowledge our own energetic detection of misalignment or complete severance of the connection. You then compound the problem by lying to yourself and whining about getting dumped. You have told yourself this lie so much you have almost started to believe it. The phrase "Love Hurts" comes to mind. Internal acceptance of any lie that reduces your power and accountability has a double whammy effect because it increases insecurity, reduces your power and creates fertile soil for you to have the same experience repeatedly.

Despite your ego not liking *how* it was handled

by the other person, be honest with yourself. Did you really not notice something was off or missing? Did it really get pass you that the relationship was misaligned, not supporting your purpose of joy and in need of repair or severing? You cannot get mad that the other person in some ways did your work for you. The question to ask yourself is, *"What prevented me from speaking up and addressing the disconnect?"* Fear of being alone? Fear of having to play the dating game again? Fear of failure? Fear of what others might think if we ended? What? Then ask yourself, *"Why is it that after the other person took action, I feel the need to play victim or vilify them for living their truth—regardless of how I might disagree with their choices?"*

Speaking of anxiety associated with other people's choices, the next chapter will discuss the importance of "holding space" when we do not agree with other people's choices and vice versa. Chapter 13 outlines how even the seeming heartache we experience serves our purpose if we allow it to. If you have freshly experienced the end of a relationship applying these chapters to that experience will reduce anger, resentment and other negative emotions. While we will never be immune to the disappointment of a failed relationship — we are now able to see it for what it really is — just a misaligned connection.

You Are Not Refreshing — Family and Friends

CHAPTER ELEVEN

You Are Not Refreshing — Family and Friends

A PERSON'S CHILDREN, SIBLINGS and other family members can look completely different from each other physically. One can have lighter complexion, hair and eyes while others have darker attributes. Some in the family could be short while others tall. This is because the individual soul has drawn its own unique composition of genetic *physical* traits. Similarly, the *personality, energy or spiritual disposition* that we are can differ greatly from members of our family. Your personality may be more heart-driven and emotionally intuitive while members of your family seem to be more mentally-driven and less emotionally inclined. You might be more creative and others more analytical, talkative and social instead of quiet and reserved. The iterations of composition are endless!

Each person has selected a unique spirit

disposition or personality through which they experience our world. To have balance would mean not judging or expecting them to be like you while also not diluting or trying to squeeze your essence to fit a mold.

The more you go within to connect with and embody your authentic essence, it is possible that members of your family may feel insulted or dishonored by your resulting individuality and departure from the expected mold. "Are you really going to dishonor us by marrying someone that __________?" "What do you mean you no longer want to do __________ for a living — it's what we all have done!" "If you are gay or lesbian, you are no longer a part of this family!" Despite the pain you feel, they actually do not mean to cause you harm.

Unfortunately, they are laden with binders that have conditioned them to believe that *their* personal value depends on other people living *their* truth and purpose. Dependence on people or entities outside of our being portrays lack of self-awareness. Their mistreatment of you reflects what is going on inside of them. They live so extrinsically –largely under the control of external ideals and customs – that they have not yet awakened to their own true heart, spirit and purpose.

Since humans tend to give love how they prefer to receive it they consequently seek to exert similar control over others through enforced ideals. This is why when you deviate from their expectation, it creates turmoil for them and behavior unbecoming a parent, sibling, grandparent or cousin. Even as they might be triggered by your choices, believe it or not your self-love and courage to live intrinsically is benefitting them as well!

People who are overly judgmental eventually learn through experience that allowing their emotional state to be easily and significantly impacted by the decisions and behavior of others is pointless and unnecessarily painful. Eventually, when they learn to stop *expecting* and *judging* the behaviors of others their quality of life will improve. You will be grateful you were able to play a role just by courageously doing you! Meanwhile, it is critical to remember their negative and seemingly un-loving behavior toward you does not necessarily depict their love for you. Another person's behavior is never about us. Rather, it reflects their current energetic state which has been molded and conditioned by mental binders usually steeped in fear.

As you go within, finding increased joy and ability to remain in personal power and alignment with your heart, you will crave more positive stimuli and association with others that similarly prioritize intrinsic fulfillment. Conversely, you will also notice increased discomfort in the presence of friends or family whose energy comprises negativity, self-pity, fixation with impressing others or over-emphasis on money. These things are not necessarily wrong in themselves and there is no judging another. However, when you see a person struggling with these your heart goes out and you naturally want to help.

When the uneasy feeling that represents lack of vibrational alignment arises, before trying to help remember how energy works. They may also feel frustrated by your positivity and empowered energy! You may wonder how can a person get a negative sensation from positivity and good intentions? This can happen because experiencing your positivity, personal strength, love and appreciation for yourself can be a stark reminder of the *absence* of such within themselves.

If they are seeking awareness they might be encouraged and uplifted by your presence and what you may have to share. However, if they are not yet seeking, then otherwise positive energy and thoughts can have a chafing effect because it is not in resonance with their current state. As much as you love them and wish for them to also experience their true power, value and purpose of greater joy and abundance, it is *their* life — not yours! Discernment in this area will come with time.

Do not take the fact that you might not be refreshing to them personally, for this is a growth opportunity for you as well! Not being energetically aligned does not mean any love is lost. Now comes the time where you learn *to hold space*. Holding space does as much good for you as it does for them. When holding space, you maintain a positive yet neutral disposition toward them and the situation, realizing it is not your place or even within your power to *bring* them to the place you are. They will go within to find their purpose and power when they reach that part of their soul journey. If the friction is great, you may decide to refrain from overly seeking out their company. Doing so is to ignore the *current* reality of your energetic states and can add undue stress to you both. Note, this does not mean giving them the cold shoulder either. Holding space is keeping a warm, loving and friendly yet *neutral* disposition with confidence that when your frequencies are in closer resonance, you both will feel the draw to mingle again.

The following are two examples of holding space in rather extreme circumstances. The first is associated with my being disowned by my family and the vast majority of my friends due to differing beliefs. The second can be observed in a letter I wrote to my mother and three siblings after the passing of my father.

Most notable about this letter is I sent it 3 years *after* my mother and siblings considered me dead to them. When I say they regard me as dead, I mean literally life and death has not moved them to speak to me! When my firstborn and now four-year-old son was born, there was no phone call, text or any expressed interest in meeting the new grandson and nephew. Also, when my one-year-old daughter was born, same thing — zero communication. Even when my father passed there was no effort to connect.

I was raised in an extreme fundamentalist Christian religion. What does that mean? Essentially it is an extreme and literal interpretation and enforcement of the bible. To refresh your memory from the introduction, while the denomination was mainstream Christianity, that is where any semblance of normalcy ends. Virtually *any* personal development or seeking of fulfillment outside of working to further the interests of the religion was strongly discouraged or outright banned. We could not participate in school sports or extra-curricular activities, or attend college, celebrate holidays or birthdays, date for fun, wear facial hair or even maintain friendships with anyone *not* in the religion. And if you no longer wanted to be in the religion you are permanently cut off from all friends and family!

Some have said that the easiest way to distinguish a religion from a cult is what happens when a person tries to leave. When a person chooses to no longer practice *religion* there is no institutional change to their personal life and relationships. However, when a person decides they no longer want to be a part of a *cult* they will effectively undergo their own death while still alive. Public announcements are made far and wide and all members are forbidden to even speak to the individual. This applies also to immediate family members. Extreme religions and cults manipulate and control through fear, shame, guilt, behavior control, emotional control and mind control.

I had never heard of someone awakening, standing in their truth and exiting the religion. Growing up we would frequently hear the announcement of someone being "disfellowshipped" or kicked out due to committing some supposedly "grave sin" as they called it. These grave sins included sex before or outside of marriage, smoking, gambling, being gay or lesbian, overdrinking, or even getting a tattoo. Yes, those are actual reasons people are institutionally cut off from their entire universe of friends and family for six months to several decades depending on their efforts to gain favor for re-admittance. Unworthy of any contact, individuals that were kicked out were largely considered 'victims who fell prey to Satan.' As such, these individuals were almost always immediately working hard to gain enough favor to get back in.

I was different. I had committed no "grave sins." I was not kicked out. I left!

As a person deeply connected to heart and spirit, it was only a matter of time before I would evolve out of extreme control and captivity! When I realized what my beloved religion was, I was devastated and sick to my stomach. My heart ached for the millions of innocent people deprived of free will and unwittingly in captivity. I explained how my beliefs had changed, declared love for all of my friends and family and exited! Included in my exit letter posted to social media in 2015 was *respect* for everyone else's right to remain faithful to principles *they* held dear and believed to be true. I also stated that I would not take their shunning of me personally. I understood how they believed their lives are at stake and that shunning me is a requirement of the religion.

In addition to losing my immediate and extended family, thousands of friends accumulated over a lifetime in various cities instantly vanished from my life. My wife and I watched our social media accounts drop by the hundreds every hour in real-time as the news spread. Remember the viral gender reveal I mentioned in chapter 5? There were comments asking why there were no black family in the video. The reason is that I lost my family and entire universe of relationships and several of my newer connections were unable to make it.

In hindsight, I remember how the religion would flip-flop tightening, loosening, then re-tightening its "disfellowship" policy in the case of immediate family members. It is as if they would relax the policy to keep people from being overwhelmed with losing family that were kicked out. Later they would re-tighten the policy after reports of family members that are still in being influenced to live more freely or the kicked-out person lacking the incentive to come back! Nonetheless, when I was in the religion and someone I loved was kicked-out I made it a point to express and show my love and support for them.

Hard-wired to live intrinsically by the heart, I hold space for the friends and family whom I may never have a relationship with again. My life since exiting has been fuller and happier than ever. My capacity to love and appreciate my fellow human beyond any fixed ideals or bias is greatly expanded. Having members of my childhood immediate family in my life are a distant second to having a complete heart that is able to love the world and myself unconditionally and without bias.

Although my father was not a fixture in my life because my parents divorced when I was about three, I went to see him every few years or so throughout my adulthood. My siblings rarely went to visit him either because he was never in the religion or they simply had no interest. My father died in the spring of 2018 which was about three years after I left the religion. Little did I know at the time that my random trip to visit him in January of 2018 would be the last time he would see any of his children before he passed just four months later.

Given the significance of his death, I felt moved to share details of the last bit of time Dad got to spend with at least one of his kids and a new grandson. While I may never fully understand the man or the inner emotions of my siblings for that matter, there was a strong heartfelt desire to recollect and share the experience as best I could with my family. Although there was no response from my mother, one of my brothers informed me that she read it and forwarded to all of my siblings.

Regarding the topic of holding space as you read the letter remember:

1. **My father had no active role in my life as a child or an adult. Instead of taking this personally, I hold space.**

2. **My siblings and mother consider me dead to them, not even worthy of a "hello." I do not take this personally, I hold space.**

Letter Written to my Estranged Mother and Three Siblings after the Death of My Father: (Names have been removed)

July 7, 2018

Hello Mom,

I have been thinking about sharing this for a while since our father passed two months ago. Can you please forward to (siblings) my re-counting the last several hours Dad spent with any of his family before he passed? I have also attached pictures.

We all know how out of sight out of mind works. Since Dad had not been a fixture in our lives it was rather easy to forget he was out there somewhere. I have seen Dad approximately 4-5 times in my adulthood. I usually made a trip to see him 1-2 times every five or six years since the age of 21. However, this latest gap had been the longest. Yana's (wife) father also was not a part of her life. In 2012 (5 years into our marriage) I took Yana and her mother to Brazil to see her father and grandfather. Yet somehow, 11 years had passed since the last time I had seen my father!

We will be married 11 years in June. Although I had spoken to Dad a few times over the years, Yana had never met him. When Colton was born, and I felt that father/son love and connection it particularly hit me I was long over-due for a visit. I thought 'Colton has to meet his grandfather while we still have him! And Dad must meet and hold his youngest grandbaby before it is too late.' However, "life" would cause another two years to elapse until the feeling became especially strong for me earlier this year. I told Yana we must make a trip! I wanted her to meet my father. And I especially wanted Dad and Colton to know each other. (This is proving much harder to write than I expected.)

I called Dad and after our usual small-talk I told him we wanted to come visit him and asked if he would like that. He immediately said yes, when! I told him I would keep him posted but we were thinking the following week. We made travel arrangements to Chicago so we could see other family and friends.

Arrival

As I drove down the street, I had an eerie feeling. This is my father's stomping ground. Sort of hard to explain. We all go about our regular lives in suburbs of TX, Chi, ATL and now China. But this non-descript Milwaukee street is where our father has spent decades of his life. Largely alone. Coming and going. Doing whatever he does with his time. Alone. The street could have been any other street in the Midwest or even Chicago. I wondered if any inside the neighboring houses and buildings were acquainted with him or valued his presence.

I didn't know how he would look since it had been so long since I last saw him. If anything has always been the case with Dad – it is that he is always handsome. This time was no different. When he opened the door, I am immediately struck by his handsomeness and brilliant golden/red skin tone. We all inherited decent complexion, but Dads was on another level. Look at the pictures and see how he almost glows! With piercing green eyes, clean shave and freshly cut hair he looked me over in amazement. He gave me a hug and said something like, "it looks like you gained weight!" I was like 'yep, happy married life does that! "I'm only 10lbs more than the last time you saw me, but it seems most of my weight first goes to my face!" He asked how old I was; when I told him – he said 41! I guess just as I freeze the age of children and those younger than me, Dad's surprise implicated he did the same! I told him we can visit just the two of us, then I would go get Yana and Colton from the car. As I follow him up the stairs, I couldn't help but think, "how is my 75-year-old father going to keep ascending these steps by himself as he ages?" His unit is simply decorated. One couch against the wall on your left as you enter and another facing you on the far wall. There is a small TV with rabbit ear antennas sitting on a crate in the center facing the couch on the left. Behind the TV was a chair against the third wall, which helped form the hallway to a bedroom and a bathroom at the end.

After chatting, I ask him if he is ready to meet his grandson and daughter-in-law and if I may go get them from the car? "Yeah," he obliges and goes down with me. He gave Yana a hug and gazed at Colton in even more amazement than he did me! Colton quietly gazes back at him from Yana's arms. Dad asked Colton's age (2), we also tell him he is lefty like both his parents and his grandfather! We then head upstairs to his unit.

We all sit down, and Yana puts Colton on the ground to walk around. Dad seems mesmerized watching Colton randomly frolicking like 2-year-olds do when allowed to be on their own two feet. Dad just quietly watches him. Eventually, Dad turns his attention to me and mentions the gray in my beard. I reminded him I look 10 years younger when clean-shaven and that I often go back and forth. I told him he is looking great and that he seems to take good care of himself.

At one point, Colton ran into a bedroom Dad apparently used as an office, den or reading room. In the office, there are stacks of periodicals, a recent paper and a round table. I note the balance of his interests according to his reading material. The magazines included Fortune, National Geographic, Ebony, People and others. Business and investing, nature and human interests. What struck me the most about his office were the pictures of us.... His family. His children. They crowd a single small round table like a mini shrine. There were framed pics and a glass "S" shaped multi-picture frame that included 80's pics of us that Mom must have sent him. There are older pics too. I especially recall one picture of Dad and Sister 1) because I do not recall ever seeing it before and 2) it was the only picture of Dad with just one of his children. While he loved us all it was clear he had only one baby girl; and she was special!

As Dad got acquainted with Yana, I recall the simplicity and incisiveness of his chosen phraseology: "Of what genetic disposition are you?" This jumped out at me because Yana and I were recently discussing both of our ancestry DNA results and how her results might require a new response when people ask her what she was. She used to just say "Brazilian" since that is where she was born. When people ask "what are you" they are trying to ascertain the genetic makeup that causes a person to look as they do. When we each did the DNA test Yana learned her dominant gene is Greek, followed by Italian and some other stuff. There was actually no "Brazilian" listed– which was surprising to Yana btw.

Yana answered Dad stating her dominant genetic make-up is Greek, while Brazil is her birth country. The sharp question and Yana's response allowed Dad to instantly glean the genetic make-up of his grandson and new daughter-in-law! It is a small thing, but you just don't hear people phrase this question so succinctly and accurately! Dad immediately then asked Yana: "do you speak Portuguese?" Yana replied yes as well as in Spanish. I then told Dad Colton will be tri-lingual at a minimum. Since my twenties I have wanted to learn Portuguese for business and because it sounds cool. I also took advanced Spanish in high school. I then shared with Dad what I learned in my DNA results. While I was 51% various African tribes - no shock there as I'm the most chocolate in the family - the composition of the other 46% was surprising. Most of my European genes are Britain instead of Ireland as we all assumed. To which Dad said, "Really!"

Dad with Colton and Overall Vibe

We asked Colton to come close to Dad and say "hi," give him a hi-five and hug. Shockingly, Colton not only obliged but also willingly sat on Dad's lap! He typically takes much longer to warm up to men. It seemed like Colton recognized Dad's energy; and someone important to him. I wondered if Colton's subconscious energy or vibes detected and comprehended the weight of the moment. They say only 7% of human communication is verbal and 93% non-verbal. This is not just body language or facial expression; it encompasses our energy and vibrational frequency.

Dad's demeanor and overall energy was warm and peaceful. Yana repeatedly told me how pleasant he was to be around. He was tender and sweet to Colton whom also enjoyed his company.

Dad's Health

As you all might recall, Dad seems to have developed a stomach issue that can intermittently cause him to repeatedly burp. As we were chatting alone before I went to get Yana and Colton from the car Dad said something like: "what did you eat, you want a mint or something?" LOL. I cracked up. Who knows what I had for breakfast at the hotel – probably an omelet with many onions and garbage in it! Anyhow, I appreciated Dad's transparency and took it as a sign of endearment. Like two friends that could say anything to each other. It also gave me the platform to be transparent back regarding his burping. Deep down I have always believed he could control it– more on that when I discuss our trip to the grocery store. Anyhow, I seized the opportunity to mirror his transparency and told him I would pop a mint if he would get the burping under control. I encouraged him saying I know he can do it as the mind controls all and is powerful – and that his mind is especially so considering we've all heard how smart he was in school. He agreed to the deal. And can you believe that for our entire visit there was no more! Until the grocery store but there was a reason which I will discuss later.

Deeper Conversation and Family

During our very pleasant time together I asked Dad if he had any mood swings or symptoms associated with bipolar and schizophrenia. He seemed to play amnesia or could have been a little embarrassed by the question. I said, "although I was very young, I understood that it was symptoms associated with these two conditions that helped cause the divorce." He then engaged and said he hadn't had mood swings, or anything associated with those symptoms in a long time. Judging by his calm peaceful demeanor I believe he was telling the truth. I also suspect that as the mind slows with age, such busy thoughts or mental over-activity likely do dissipate.

I asked if he ever thought about us. He said Yes! I asked him what sort of thoughts come to mind, do you envision us around the house altogether, on a vacation, etc.? I do not recall his answer. He may not have answered due to a distraction or something. I then asked him a very general life question: After 75 years on this earth, do you have any regrets? He immediately said, "I wish I would have put forth more effort to stay married to your mother." That was enough said, and I did not probe him further on this.

I shifted our dialogue to the present because I did not want him to feel an inordinate amount of shame associated with the divorce or him not being a present father. He has suffered enough with a life of near solitude. I encouraged him that the beautiful benefit of having 20/20 hindsight is that it moves us to adjust the present which directly improves our *current and future days. I showed him pictures of Colton in my phone and on Instagram. He seemed impressed that I could have such a collection of pics in the phone! I told him there are ways for him to easily see a whole lot more pics and that we can text each other pictures.*

I looked at his phone and it was very basic and not a smartphone. He did not have my number or hardly any numbers programmed. He was using a paper list with key phone numbers which could easily get lost. So, I programmed my phone number and taught him how to quickly dial me, our grandma and his two brothers. I told him we could also look into getting him a smartphone and perhaps upgrading his plan to include data. This seemed intimidating to him, so I didn't press, though I did look into this with his provider after we parted ways.

Grocery Run

Dad asked if I could take him to the store. We piled in the rental SUV and took a field trip. I dropped him at the entrance and Yana, Colton and I waited in the car while he did his personal shopping. He was in the store for 20 minutes then 30, 40, 50 minutes! I was getting worried but also trying to respect his space and dignity. I finally decided I better go in. I found him in a food aisle shopping. He already had some meat from the butcher, some butter and other knick-knacks in his cart. I asked him if there were any other categories he wanted to hit – cereal, veggie produce, bread, drinks etc. We added milk, bread, tomato sauce, soda pop and a few more things then went to check out. While waiting in line he mysteriously burped – which he had not done for the last 3-4 hours. There may have been some anxiety regarding his ability to pay for everything. The belching was getting noticed by others. I whispered to him, "Dad, you got this, get it under control." Then he almost immediately stopped burping. The support, confidence and encouragement felt warm to him, perhaps eased his anxiety and he just stopped. I paid for his groceries and we went home. We stocked his kitchen together while Colton and Yana chilled in the family room. He thanked me profusely. We hugged and I assured him I loved him.

It was time for us to get back on the road. I reminded him he has control over the rest of his life. The past is the past. If he wants his family in his life he has only to try – we are right in his phone. I also mentioned that we should try to see each other more often.

In the car Yana and I discussed the possibility of taking him in and making our next house one with an external guest suite. But I also knew this would not necessarily be an improvement for him. Yes, he would have our love. But he cannot experience that 24/7. He has been doing things his way on his terms living where he wanted for all his life. Such an extreme change can often send morale the other way. Yet I knew the time would eventually come that we would want to get him into a nice assisted living center he could pick.

Summary and Feelings

The visit was very nice and sad and painful for me. It was hard for me to see my father living alone with virtually no one in his life. I wondered what he had been doing the last 11+ years since I last saw him. I wondered about the last 38 years since Mom and he divorced. Day in.... day out.... with no family, no close friends, no girlfriend (yes, I asked), not even a pet.

When his brother called me to let me know Dad had passed, I felt enormous sadness along with a measure of relief. I hated how Dad was living. It then immediately crossed my mind that perhaps our visit provided a measure of closure for him and he was ready to go. Remember my strong urgency to go see him? You know how they say twins have been proven to be spiritually or telepathically connected and can sense issues with each other. Perhaps this was something similar we never know. Anyhow, Dad felt real love from me and also my being proud to be his son regardless of the past. His brains and athleticism are among the many gifts he passed along to us. He met his youngest prodigy. He had been living a tough and lonely life. There likely was not much left for him in this life.

I have never felt negative feelings or resentment toward Dad. Whether because I was so young when they divorced or because resentment and judgment are simply not parts of my character – or perhaps both. But my heart goes out to my older siblings who were old enough to remember losing him. For example, I just learned this year about what happened

152

when Mom and we all came looking for him after he had not come home in several days. My heart sank particularly for my brothers because they were plenty old enough to feel rejected and likely endured great pain.

I hope time has healed your wounds and that you not only have peace and closure – but closure even with love in your heart for the man that none of us knew or understood, yet all have strong traces of. I hope you can comprehend that Dad's choices had absolutely nothing to do with you. This is evidenced by the fact that Dad remained alone. Alone in the most literal sense! To say he had a challenged existence is an understatement. We all have kids and know firsthand how fulfilling being co-creators and raising children can be. Ask yourself what must have been going on within his soul for him to willingly forfeit what is unanimously considered one of the most rewarding aspects of life!

How sad for him he missed out on observing and shaping his four children's progression to adulthood and eventually having children of their own. Any pain or supposedly less than desirable life we think we might have experienced by his absence pales compared to Dad's journey. I also wonder if his gastro issues may have somehow been self-imposed as punishment for abandoning us. It is like he was in conflict and did not want to leave us but also internally needed to learn loneliness and pain. I just know it was interesting that he could instantly stop the gastro issues. Yet I also understand his stomach was the physical catalyst for his death – internal bleeding. It could also just be a coincidence that a loving visit from his children enabled him to temporarily lose the gastro issues. Our physical health is inextricably intertwined with our emotional state, unresolved issues, etc. I just wish I understood what value or lessons. Dad's inner self might have been trying to learn by manifesting the life he chose for himself. Maybe someday we will have all the answers. Maybe we won't. Maybe someday it simply will not matter or will not be called to mind.

But I wanted you all to know that I saw and heard firsthand that Dad loved us! He loved Mom! He never stopped loving any of us! He even honored us in the ways he knew how.

Love,

Aaron

PART FOUR

Awakening to Your Power

Are You Discounting Yourself

CHAPTER TWELVE

Are You Discounting Yourself

I HAVE AN MBA. An MBA, as in Master of Business Administration. Does that sound posh and swanky to you? I hope not! Before you think this is some form of fake self-deprecation, please allow me to explain. I am fairly ho-hum about it. No, that's not the right term. I suppose there are parts of me that are somewhat ashamed of it. Ok, that definitely came out wrong! I personally invested two years and $120,000 — I am *not* ashamed of my MBA. Let's try this again. I sometimes forget I have an MBA. That is more like it. I forget I have an MBA not because it was easily accomplished or a forgettable achievement. Quite the contrary, actually!

Obtaining an MBA from a top business school like SMU Cox School of Business, while working full-time and trying to be a "present" husband and friend, was one of the most challenging things I have ever undertaken. Compounding the difficulty was that I had never attended college. Executive MBA Programs place more emphasis on candidates having proven business leadership and documented success than simply undergraduate studies. You might be thinking — shouldn't achieving an MBA without an undergrad result in *more* pride of the accomplishment instead of less? Perhaps, but this just was not the case with me.

When I journeyed to my within, things began to make sense. Attending higher education at 37 years old with no prior college meant my life thus far had been devoid of early academic aspirations and subsequent chest-puffing pride and sense of accomplishment and entitlement typically attributed to higher education. Some reasons why higher education was never an option for me were covered in the previous chapter. Before I attended business school, my mold had been long cast and I was already successful. As discussed in Chapter 6, by 23 I had already manifested an extremely successful and high-income career. By 25 years old, I was making half-a-million dollars per year. I built a million-dollar custom home and stocked the garage with cool cars. I had always believed and even personified the idea that:

Higher education was neither required for success nor should it be a barometer of a person's aptitude or likelihood for success.

With my success why did I even bother to pursue

an MBA? It is often said the more you know the less you realize you know. Though I had succeeded in business, helping hundreds of companies, closed countless multi-million-dollar deals and also was a founding member of a startup in my mid-twenties, I had thus far never been the founding CEO responsible for all aspects of a business. There was a nagging awareness I would someday grow a business from concept to fiscally successful company and I wanted to close any exposed flanks by learning each aspect of business in greater detail. Most Executive MBA candidates make the investment of time and money to achieve certain income objectives or get to the next career ladder rung. Since my income was already $500k-$1m+ annually the only pot of gold at the end of my MBA rainbow would have to be created by me through higher performance or creating my own company. That I had no immediately extrinsic motivation for getting the MBA was rather unique.

Although I have always been a strong proponent of living intrinsically, I cannot say that my reasons for pursuing an MBA were 100% intrinsic. In the deep recesses of my psyche was a mild craving for external validation or assimilation. It cannot be overemphasized the amount of pressure societal and environmental norms and customs exert upon us. As social creatures, we have a strong yearning to assimilate and align within social groups which is not a bad thing. We must conform to certain societal norms such as laws or there would be anarchy. And we enjoy and appreciate the support and comradery of the social community. The problem is when we begin erringly discounting ourselves, accomplishments, natural gifts or even physical attributes as *shortcomings* that have missed some idealized external mark.

Take the fact that one of my underlying motivations for getting an MBA was some sort of tangible evidence I had paid my dues, was disciplined and accomplished. Really? I had tuned in to my aptitudes, applied myself and iterated at such a rapid pace that I was delivering substantial value to corporations and personal wealth for myself and my family by the time most people were starting an entry-level job fresh out of college. What more validation could I have possibly needed? What can I say? Humans are highly social creatures. Sometimes we think we just want to be like everybody else and fit in.

The very things about ourselves that we under-value, other people might admire and be inspired by. During my graduate studies, I met a classmate who not only had the typical undergrad degree but another advanced degree as well. One day he was complaining how "unfair" it seemed that rappers can be worth so much with no higher education while there are people like him with a repertoire of degrees earning commensurately little. The cloth my classmate was cut from is that of the prioritization of formal education above all else. Yet there was a part of him that marveled at the idea that people were amassing substantial wealth with so little formal education. You could say his "fixed" mindset was having a head-on collision with the other side of his aura which happened to be very growth mindset.

I knew he was about to undergo a massive transformation. He was in the midst of teaching himself a life-lesson right before my eyes that would render his formerly "fixed mindset" a ginormous black eye expanding his perspective forever. And I would unwittingly play a critical role. In the next few minutes he learned that despite me not having an undergraduate, I was earning colossal income. Light bulbs went off in his head and you could almost see his mind-opening. I cannot take all the credit for the ensuing growth he would undergo over the next six months we studied together, but I felt honored to play a role.

It seems we were energetically drawn to each other. His subconscious mind led him to me for an object lesson that his soul was ready to learn, namely that everything in life is not as fixed, linear and quantitative as they might seem. We grow more from exposure to energy and concepts foreign to us than we do from things we already have our arms around. On more than one occasion he told me how much he appreciated and learned from my growth-mindset and application of emotional intelligence to deliver substantial business outcomes. I benefited from his academic rigor and excellence having completed two prior degrees. It was such a great pairing. I may not have graduated without him! A year after graduation he reported back to me that he "got out of his head" and transitioned from product management to sales where he more than doubled his income and was thriving!

I may not hold having an MBA on my sleeve because I have experienced and truly believe we are all so much more than our physical experiences, assets and education, but I am appreciative for the Cox School of Business allowing me the opportunity to experience such a challenging, diverse and altogether awesome Executive MBA program.

If you have an imbalanced view about some aspect of yourself or are overly seeking to live up to external ideals, you might be robbing the world of your best gifts. In the moment you are shrinking back, assimilating or feeling inferior about something unique to you or even an accomplishment you deem insignificant, pay attention to your body. The feelings inside your body and prodding of the heart are like your very own masterclass. Not only does thinking less of yourself feel like crap but being inauthentic is also unnecessarily hard work!

Take a look at this picture of my son and me. If you look closely, you might be able to discern the 2-year-old boy is struggling to use the fork with his right hand because he is a lefty like both of his parents. Since all the kids are right-handed, he is learning firsthand how much of a struggle it is to try to be something he is not in effort to be like everyone else. As he grows into himself, we hope he learns to appreciate left-handedness is one of his gifts and should be celebrated not hidden!

Ask yourself, "In what areas might I be discounting myself due to perceived societal norms or expectations?" As we learn to go within frequently and ask *why*, often we not only expand our comprehension, but we grow in unconditional love and appreciation for our uniquely important essence.

One of the most common areas people discount themselves is the area of physical appearance and aging. Why is it that people are so quick to discount their own traits while preferring features they do not have? Darker races perm their hair to straighten, whereas lighter skin races get perms to curl their hair. Darker races used to think light skin was better, and lighter skin races spend billions of dollars on tanning. Lighter skin races are known to get lip injections and darker races used to tease each other about their full lips.

In the western world getting older is so negatively regarded that nearly everyone seeks to avoid or hide signs of aging such as gray hair like the plague. Ironically, if you consider the hairs closely you will notice gray hairs are usually much thicker, stronger and have more sheen. If you've ever tried to pluck a gray hair you learned they are much more difficult to uproot than their beloved pigmented counterparts. Have you ever wondered why? Do you think this is coincidental? While other physical aspects might seem to deteriorate with age, this particular one by all empirical measures seems to get stronger. Could gray hair be the one qualitatively visible indicator that aging may not be such a bad thing?

We discussed earlier that as we age, we become more intrinsically anchored and driven. We also become more empathetic, accepting of others and cooler tempered. Are there not disproportionately fewer bitterly hateful and angry 80-year-old people? Perhaps gray hair is one of nature's physical indicators that progression towards our transition is actually beautiful and not something that should be viewed with disdain. Of course, we will never really know until we go – but realities are often not what we perceive.

Regardless of the topic, the realization of our greatest potential happens at the intersection of maximum appreciation *with* aspiration. They are not mutually exclusive.

We must find reasons to genuinely appreciate where we currently are while aspiring to grow and expand.

Be careful of saying "I will be enough when," "I will be accomplished after," "I will be happy and fulfilled when this or that happens." Requiring some external or future condition, achievement or event for self-love reduces our power and adds friction to our current state. Low appreciation also squanders precious time which is the most valuable thing we all have. However, when we flip this on its head and allow real appreciation to flow even during a supposedly unfavorable state, the emanating positive energy will propel us to manifest ever greater optimism, joy and results.

Try weaving deep appreciation into every aspect of your life — your body and physical health, relation-ships, career as well as personal goals. By doing so you more fully enjoy the journey *and* the destination. Don't be one of those people that refuses to take pictures until they lose weight but have also been 'trying to lose weight' for years. Do you really want to blink and realize you have missed living because you were too critical and unappreciative of yourself mainly due to comparing yourself to other people or society at large? The most important opinion of you is your own. Self-love is not unhealthy ego. Rather, it is the basis from which all other love is possible. Preoccupation with how *other* people view you is unhealthy ego. And since everything we experience reflects what we feel inside, if we do not unconditionally love ourselves experiencing unconditional love from others will prove elusive.

If you struggle with low self-esteem, here is an interesting thing to remember when you are discounting your worth. Your brilliance is so great that you have written, directed, edited, were a cinematographer and starred in some of the most epic movies ever created. And you did them all in just one take! Not even legendary Hollywood filmmakers can better the incredible motion pictures you singlehandedly create every night when you fall asleep and dream! If you can unconsciously produce at this level, imagine what you can do with deliberate effort. The only difference between dreams and what happens when we are awake is a conscious decision. Congratulations on your progression to becoming unbounded, whereby you no longer discount yourself with self-defeating thoughts!

The Darker the Brighter—
How Anxiety Serves You

CHAPTER THIRTEEN

The Darker the Brighter— How Anxiety Serves You

YOU HEAR IT in conversation. You see it all over social media. You even see it on people's faces. There is no escaping the preponderance of anxiety that grips so many. Nobody likes to feel anxious. Anxiety leads to fear and fear leads to more anxiety. No one likes to feel uncertain about their livelihood or income, health or romantic relationship. In addition to our own personal concerns, 24-hour access to news piles on things like the economy, global warming, war, localized violence, natural disasters, civil unrest and more. In this over-exposed and over-informed era anxiety can be and often *is* the most significant impediment to our purpose of joy and fulfillment. We have all heard and experienced how fear can be crippling.

Think back to a situation where you had to perform and you were well prepared – whether performing in a school play, a presentation at work or a speech. Now think about another situation where you were completely *unprepared.* While you may have felt a measure of anxiety in both instances, you probably felt significantly more anxiety when you were unprepared! There are three key points about anxiety that when understood can condition and prepare you for anything you might face. As always, it is only when we deliberately go within, comprehend and connect the dots that life lessons are integrated allowing us to level up and proceed to the next challenge.

Considering anxiety is such a formidable impediment to our happiest existence, you might want to write down your answers to these questions to help your lesson become more deeply integrated into your consciousness.

The first point is that 99% of anxiety is associated with an event or outcome that has either not happened or is in the past.

"I think I'm going to fail this test." "How could I have done that?" "I will never find someone that loves me." "I'm going to get evicted." "I am going to get fired." "What if I don't succeed?" Anxiety causes fear, and the actual purpose of fear is to alert us to *immediate* danger and the need for either fight or flight.

Ask yourself: "What is currently causing me

to feel anxious and is it immediately dangerous or life-threatening?"

____

____

____

Is there a lion about to eat you or a car about to crash through your house as you read these words? When loaded down with anxieties, we are essentially walking around suffering in our *imagination*. You are also planning to suffer twice. We suffer the first time by having such a great imagination that the body feels like we are experiencing the problem. You suffer a second time if it happens. Most, unfortunately, when fixated on the anxiety it is more likely to happen because the mind gets what it dwells or focuses on. This is another reason anxiety scares us so much; dreaded outcomes seem guaranteed to happen because we have a history of unwittingly ensuring it!

Be in *this* moment. You are alive. You are safe. The event or situation so heavily weighing you down has either not occurred yet, or is in the past. Allowing it to inordinately consume you has a ripple effect that lowers your frequency, your physical energy, creativity and motivation. These compound the problem by impeding and stifling your ability to positively and creatively counteract or resolve the matter.

In periods of high anxiety, resist the urge to direct all your attention to the issue and how you will resolve it. Doing so keeps you in the energy of the *problem*. At this time it is more critical than ever to do things that make you feel joy and replenishment. In parallel, deeply reflect upon and hold sincere gratitude for all the good in your life. After your energy or spirit is of a lighter and higher vibrational frequency, you can now give attention to the problem.

The key is to *observe* the challenge or situation that is causing you anxiety. We observe it because observing creates a very different feeling than experiencing it. When we observe, we are able to think and perform without the encumbrance of personal emotion. When it comes to anxiety the primary emotion is almost always crippling fear. The next two points are my favorite aspects about anxiety. Yes, I said favorite, and something tells me you may love them too!

The second lesson is that your worst experiences can greatly improve the rest of your life!

I love this truth. Go inside and recount how this has proven true for you. Think about some challenging or painful situation or event you endured; a bad relationship, a job you hated, or even the unbearably painful initial period of grieving the passing of someone you loved. The suffering and anxiety were so immense that it seems to have left a permanent mark forever changing you. And it does! The question is whether you will allow that mark to serve or hinder you.

The greater the pain, the greater it's capacity to serve you. This is true because when you finally get beyond the enormous pain or suffering you cannot help but profoundly notice the absence of it! "I am so glad I am no longer in the darkness I experienced when I first lost my loved one, in a one-sided or abusive relationship, have to go every day to a job I hate or was grossly underappreciated," etc. Because of the pain you went through or load you once carried, other problems and challenges seem small by comparison and you more easily remain content and happy. In a way, you are now better off than others that might not have ever experienced what you have endured; they require much more to feel internally appreciative. In this way, massively challenging or painful experiences have the power to literally brighten the rest of our days!

As a personal example, I used to occasionally get asked whether I felt angry or bitter for being raised in such an extreme fundamentalist religion causing me to miss out on so many things. My life had been absent of things like youth sports and activities, school dances, the ability to pick my own friends without control or guilt, celebrate birthdays and holidays, wearing a beard, going to college or even something as simple as doing what I wanted on evenings and weekends! My answer is no way, I do not have even an ounce of bitterness!

Remember that while in the religion my life did not seem terrible because I deeply believed and focused on the positives of the lifestyle. The adage "ignorance is bliss" comes to mind. Although the side effects of one awakening to the truth and what they have missed can cause intense anger, self-pity, regret and depression, it has proven to be the opposite for me. Even several years after exiting I am monumentally thankful for the simplest things in life including mental and behavioral freedom. The contrast helps me to more deeply love and enjoy life and appreciate others unconditionally and without judgment. In this way my past captivity actually serves and enhances my quality of life by making me more easily content, appreciative and also accepting of other people's beliefs and choices. Reflect upon one or more of your past deep anxieties and how they might positively affect your perception today.

The third lesson is that our ability to transmute anxieties can transform our physiological makeup to super-human levels.

As always, we will go within for our most profound lessons and growth. Think of every childhood and even adulthood hero and inspirational figure you have admired. What is the common thread across them all including the fictitious ones? What catalyzes each to step into their purpose and perform at ostensibly other-worldly levels that inspire so many? Is it not always some sort of ominously challenging obstacle, pain, suffering, tragedy or injustice? This makes perfect sense and is a law of the universe! Diamonds undergo immense pressure before becoming the hardest and most beautiful stone on earth. One does not become physically stronger than average without lifting or carrying more than average. When lifting weights, the physical load tears and breaks down muscles before building them up.

We cannot become super without being super. It is impossible to manifest mega-blessings of personal fulfillment, beautifully compatible relationships, and dream jobs being led by the same ego mind and triggered by the same fears as everyone else. Supreme abundance is ours when we learn to transmute or transform "bad" experiences or challenges into positive energy that *serves* us and eventually others by extension.

This is easier to do when we take the vantage point of observing our life. As an illustration, imagine a world whereby we all were just stones. You can pick the type of stone you want to be (i.e., Granite, Ruby, Limestone, Basalt, Marble, Jade, Onyx, Diamond, etc.). Whenever someone would pick diamond they might hear: "Um, you do realize that to be a diamond you must undergo tremendous pressure, right?" "Yes, but I don't care, I so much identify with its beauty and strength that it will be worth it!" This silly illustration makes the point well. When we imagine or *observe* instead of experience it is much easier to see the big picture and accept the required journey.

Your most painful experiences and greatest anxieties; though not deliberately selected, are required for you to become what you are meant to be. Your favorite leaders, athletes, singers, activists, artists, entrepreneurs and more did not consciously choose to be raised in orphanages, experience inordinate ridicule, rejection, poverty, abuse or tragedy. Yet they are aware and often verbalize in documentaries and interviews how outwardly negative and even tragic events of their lives were instrumental in stepping into their true purpose and ultimately enjoying a more fulfilling life.

Whether we realize it now or not, life will eventually reveal that you are in control and do not need to worry or fear. Our essence or spirit is design-engineering the experience of life. When we make conscientious effort to be heart-driven we in effect stop fighting this force and silence the mind along with its many binders resulting in a more integrated, purposeful and satisfying life.

Regardless of where you are on your journey, draw comfort in knowing a part of you is in complete control making things like self-pity and regret imaginary. If you are thinking this cannot be so because there are things you could not have possibly wanted to happen. What do children do when they get a boo-boo? Then what do they do when it heals? Even adults do it! The boo-boo becomes a badge of honor to show off! Not necessarily happy that it happened but show off with a sense of accomplishment they endured and are now well or even better. Is there not achievement in suffering? Is not accomplishment sweeter after sacrifice and perseverance? A job we love even more fulfilling after years of jobs we hated or were not a fit? The seemingly bad we endure 1) reminds us how strong we really are, 2) positions us to help others at the right time, and 3) makes life sweeter and enriches the soul. You may not get all the details and answers now. However, you will realize that any darkness you experience is forming you to embody your greatest expression and contribution yet!

The soul always gets what it wants.

If something you deeply desire never comes to fruition it means either your soul does not actually want it or it requires that you work through and eradicate various binders before you are able to attract it. Since 90% of our behavior or experience is derived from subconscious thought what do your interests and experiences reveal about your subconscious essence? Energy attracts its likeness. Hence, unless you want more of something in your life think twice about engaging with it. This applies to people, our conversation, TV, movies and what we read. If you feed on drama, conflict, and focus on "lack," you draw such into your journey. The eyes and ears are like windows and doors on a house. What you open them up to has the power to transform the energy inside. If you want light, ease and abundance, seek things that foster connection to your inner higher self. The journey goes within before it goes up both energetically and physically.

After going within and becoming armed with such internal awareness, instead of being 'damned' to our anxieties; we are actually '*good* if we do and *good* if we don't.' If you have been through or are in a period of significant personal suffering and/or adversity, consider yourself privileged. For everyone does not get the opportunity to experience the bliss you will know when the problem is no more. This is because the darker it gets the brighter the potential!

Your Journey, Your Sum

CHAPTER FOURTEEN

Your Journey, Your Sum

TWO BOYS ARE wrestling in the house. Loud playful voices and thumping sounds escalate as the intensity of their play increases. Their mother yells out from her bedroom, "You boys better stop roughhousing before you break something in my living room." Do you think this causes the boys to immediately stop? Not a chance! Pent up energy with surging testosterone egg them on until they hear a sound. The sound freezes them in their tracks simultaneously stopping their hearts. Mom's voice again? Nope. Dad's car in the driveway? Even scarier than that. They hear the crashing sound of one of Mom's favorite vessels shattering.

When Mom and Dad sit the boys down to figure out how the vessel was broken, what happens? You guessed it; each boy emphatically swears that it was the other one's fault! Instinctive self-preservation causes them to immediately divert responsibility to avoid having to shoulder the emotional and possibly even physical pain associated with disappointing their parents. This diversion of responsibility would not happen if they had not previously experienced the displeasure and pain associated with upsetting Mom and Dad.

Early on we develop a pattern of shifting account-ability for nearly every unpleasant experience of life. This pattern is self-defeat masquerading as self-preservation that we think benefits us. To ascribe account-ability for our bad experience to another person or entity feels better and easier than having to look in the mirror and acknowledge that we have internal work to do. In the midst of soothing and comforting ourselves we suffocate our own power and bathe in victimhood — which then becomes addictive like a drug. By the time we are adults, we possess a plethora of learned habits and coping mechanisms that diminish our power. Often our self-defeating coping mechanisms get camouflaged in perceived societally created inequities like social class, nationality, sex, race, appearance, religion, sexual orientation, height, weight and more. As discussed in chapter 13, the way we choose to see life's challenges will either be fuel to our purpose of joy and fulfillment or add to a growing collection of binders that impede it.

Equal care must also be taken to avoid unduly diverting accountability for our accomplishments and successes.

It is a good thing to feel appreciation for other people. The emotion of appreciation is one of the higher frequencies. However:

The degree to which we attribute our sum to others can also be hindering our power to realize our purpose and life we desire.

Let me illustrate. For the first ten years of my professional career, whenever reflecting upon my life's journey and achievements, I used to conclude that most of my professional life might not have happened without a certain person. His name was Dan. Dan was the CEO of a small technology consulting firm in Chicago that was one of my clients when I was a 19-year-old corporate pager communications sales representative. For you young folks, pagers were what professionals used before cell phones to keep in touch. Desiring more complex business challenges to solve, I inquired about a job and was introduced to Dan. For some reason, Dan made a special trip out of his way and interviewed me in his convertible Saab. Other than high school, I had no formal education or experience architecting technology solutions to business problems. Nonetheless, Dan felt compelled to create a position for me. I became an Inside Sales Representative where I absorbed not like a sponge – better! Within six months I had morphed into an Outside Sales Executive. I was 15-25 years younger than my four peers.

That job was my entrée into the technology

industry which I later realized is not only challenging to break into, but sales is even more so. What caused Dan to hire me? Years later I asked him this very question. His answer was something like: 'I figured if a kid can be that successful selling something as boring as pagers, he would be great selling cool technology.' While that sounds funny and may have been Dan's mental or conscious reason, I shared with him what I believed might be the subconscious heart-based reason he hired me. To make this point I took him back to when he would accompany me on my initial face-to-face meetings with clients as I began transitioning from Inside Sales to Outside Sales Executive.

We were walking down Monroe Street in downtown Chicago in the freezing cold on our way to a large law firm. Dan randomly begins to cross the street. "Dan, where are you going, the appointment is on this side!" I said after catching up to his brisk stride. He said "Did you see that homeless person up ahead on the sidewalk? I would rather not encounter such sadness on our way to see a client." At nineteen I had not yet put together that both Dan and I were empaths. Dan also had a "growth mindset," which is the opposite of a "fixed mindset."

One of the many fixed ideals of our era is 'if I do not see it being done already, I will assume it cannot be done.' This plays out commercially through inaccurate assumptions that limit the aptitudes and capabilities of women, disabled, minorities, veterans, ex-convicts and virtually anyone that is "different" than what is typically seen.

Dan internally knew that anything was possible for anyone. A person's only limitation is the force operative inside of them. Such a vibrational essence was in perfect resonance with mine. As far back as I can remember, I have always known I was my only limitation and I saw the world according to merit. I believe Dan subconsciously sensed this familiar vibration and identified parts of himself in me. It is as if our souls recognized each other, made a handshake and began collaborating. I ended up over-performing. This was the job that enabled me to buy my first house and cars, which taught me a valuable life lesson at 20 years old as referenced in chapter 4.

There was Joe, the Worldwide VP of Sales for an enterprise software company that hired me when I was twenty-three. The complexity of the software plus the fact that I would be advising senior executives including CEOs on business transformation, made Joe hiring me at 23 perhaps even more inexplicable than Dan hiring me at 19! Joe's energy was anything but the cliché egotistical sales executive. While working for Joe, I often told him how much I appreciated his approachable and empathetic nature that never seemed too busy to take a personal interest. He would often self-deprecatingly joke about his appearance saying things like:

"Aaron, with your gifts you should carry a bag and make as much money for as long as possible before even considering management. Some day you will be old, fat and bald like me and then you can manage."

Though not particularly any of those things, Joe was indeed different. He had a nicer more unassuming demeanor and stature that belied his power and achievements. Could it be that Joe also sensed aspects of himself in me? I became a top producer selling $20 million in software and consulting services over three years. As a gesture of my appreciation, I hosted Joe's retirement party at the mansion in Frisco, Texas that I bought with my earnings.

Then there was John, who hired me at 32 to work for one of the most iconic technology companies in history – IBM. Most intriguing is the way John hired me. To this day, I have never heard of a multi-million-dollar business sales executive getting hired without a face-to-face interview. So much is at stake that careful consideration is always given to ensure the selected candidate not only has the credentials but in person demonstrated ability to command a room of executives. John hired me after only two phone interviews!

Equally significant were the circumstances of my

life at the time this happened. I had just resigned from my previous employer and in the middle of a recession! I resigned in part due to interference with my then somewhat extreme religious routine. Seven years later I fortunately awakened and exited the extreme religion. However, at the time I resigned, I was standing in my truth. I was scared sick about becoming unemployed during a recession and how bad things might get. Lo and behold John hired me in record time and in this rather unorthodox 'sight unseen' way. Although John and I did not work together long, we had quite a bit in common including growth mindset, complete color-blindness, both empathetic, transparent and fun-loving. During my tenure at IBM, I set the pace globally, winning consecutive awards over seven years as well as being honored as "Best of IBM," the top 1% of 400,000 employees!

Do I value these three men and the opportunities they extended me? Absolutely! Yet, I do not view any of them as reasons for my success. I deeply appreciate them for the people they are and consider them members of my soul or spirit family. We love individuals for who and what they are, but it has become clear that accountability or attribution for our experiences in life are less about specific individuals and more about what we are energetically.

In other words, if Dan, Joe and John never

existed, my subconscious energy, soul or spirit would have drawn and collaborated with different people that embodied similar energetic resonance and mutual subconscious desire to collaborate and grow in some way. In more ways than can be penned in a single book, life beautifully teaches how interconnected we all are, working in concert without our even realizing it.

Now it is your turn! Think through some of your accomplishments. You may notice several are precipitated by the help or mercy of another; which may have caused you to attribute your success to them. Humility is a refreshing quality and also makes additional growth possible. However, balance is key! There is absolutely no discrediting of people that have been helpful in your life. The recognition of even deeper meaning and force that drew your paths enrichens the connection beyond only the mind and into the heart space. By going within and analyzing your life and patterns over time, it will become clear that your role and power is much larger and unbounded than you ever realized.

We are all architects of our own respective journey, intersecting with others where there is synergistic alignment, resonance or lessons our soul wants to learn.

Some may wonder… would not the belief that everything we need is within us negate the value of reading books or listening to what anyone else has to say? Not entirely. The value we derive from each other when we are trying to grow and expand fit into two buckets: Technical training or validation of universal truths beginning to emerge within us. Note that neither of these changes what we are. There is nothing wrong with you. Our purest expression does not need to be changed; it only needs the be discovered. In this way, we are "stimuli" to each other's discovery which only happens within.

Whether you realized it or not you are constant stimulus for others. The word "chemistry" denotes energy that is familiar or has resonance. Will people feel resonance with you for expansive positive reasons or fear-based, negative self-defeating ones? After reading this book and journeying to your personal "within" I hope you feel inspired, motivated and reminded that the happiest, most fulfilled, authentic and powerful you result from maintaining a clear connection to your heart purpose of joy, unconditional love and appreciation.

You do not have to be secularly in the arts to be the positive stimulus that uplifts those who experience you. Artistry is not as narrowly defined as many think. In my observation, anyone who enjoys contributing to the happiness of others is an artist. Some contribute their art through the imagination via what they create, the ears by what they speak, sing or write, through the hands via touch or productive work they perform and *all* of us contribute by the space of loving positive intention we hold within our hearts for each other. Whatever your favorite art form, partake and share often, remain intrinsically-driven by your heart as you shed those binders and become Unbounded!

About the Author

ARON MCCORMICK IS an author, entrepreneur, inspirational speaker and artist whose path to success and fulfillment defies societal norms and expectations in nearly every way.

Raised by a single mom on the South Side of Chicago, McCormick, since the age of 23 was one of the world's leading technology business transformation sales executives, earning millions and receiving numerous awards and distinctions. He has been honored as "Best of IBM," an award bestowed upon the top 1% of 400,000 employees, founded several companies and earned an MBA from a top business school with the rare precedent of having no prior undergraduate college degree. McCormick courageously stood up to and escaped the fundamentalist religious cult in which he was raised, resulting in loss of his universe of friends and family.

With the combination of deep empathy, wisdom, and self-made success, McCormick ignites the innate ability we all have within to decode our own answers for maximum clarity and self-actualization. Aaron has helped countless people of all backgrounds realize greater fulfillment and success in areas of career, personal power, love & relationships, sales, entrepreneurship and leadership.

Website

www.aaronmccormick.com

Instagram

@theaaronmccormick

Facebook

www.facebook.com/theaaronmccormick

Youtube

www.youtube.com/c/Unbounded

Made in the USA
Monee, IL
06 May 2020